Accounting and Financial Management in the Hotel and Catering Industry

Volume 2

Catering Times Books

The Modern Pâtissier – A
Complete Guide to Pastry Cookery   *William Barker*
The Microwave Recipe Book   *Lewis Napleton*
A Guide to Microwave Catering   *Lewis Napleton*
Catering with Meat   *J. Dando and F. Mallion*
Microbiology and Food   *B. J. Ford*
A Guide to Systemised Catering   *Lewis Napleton*
The Golden Age of British Hotels   *Derek Taylor and David Bush*
A Directory of Wines and Spirits   *Pamela Vandyke Price*
Entertaining with Wine   *Pamela Vandyke Price*
Wines and Spirits for the Caterer   *Philip Shaw*

Accounting and Financial Management in the Hotel and Catering Industry

Volume 2

Peter J. Harris, M.H.C.I.M.A., C.Dip.A.F.

Senior Lecturer, School of Hotel and Institutional Administration
Robert Gordon's Institute of Technology, Aberdeen

Peter A. Hazzard, M.Sc., F.C.M.A., A.M.B.I.M.

Senior Lecturer, School of Accountancy
Slough College of Higher Education

NORTHWOOD PUBLICATIONS LTD
London EC1V 7QA

First published 1972
Second Edition 1977

A Catering Times Book

31813028

ISBN 7198 2553 9

This book has been set in Times, printed in Great Britain by The Anchor Press Ltd, and bound by Wm Brendon & Son Ltd, both of Tiptree, Essex

PREFACE TO THE SECOND EDITION

The mechanics of accounting in the hotel and catering industry as in any other industry are only a means to an end, and the more modern approach to the consideration of the study of accounting is to place more emphasis on the end, the object being to assist management by using significant financial information.

This book (Vol 2) has been separated into two sections. Chapters 1–3 deal with the preparation of annual accounting statements. Chapters 4–15 are concerned with the presentation of accounting information to assist management in making business decisions.

The needs of students studying for hotel and catering qualifications, executives and management within the industry and the small hotelier and caterer have been carefully borne in mind throughout this work.

Volume 1 satisfies the accounting requirements of:

(a) the Hotel, Catering and Institutional Management Association (H.C.I.M.A.) Intermediate Membership Examination;

(b) the Ordinary National Diplomas (O.N.D.) in Hotel, Catering and Institutional Operations, year one; and

(c) the Hotel Book-keeping Receptionist Certificates and Diplomas.

Volume 2 satisfies the accounting requirements of:

(a) the Hotel, Catering and Institutional Management Association (H.C.I.M.A.) Final Membership Examination; and

(b) the Ordinary National Diplomas (O.N.D.) in Hotel, Catering and Institutional Operations, year two.

Volumes 1 and 2 combined, satisfy the accounting requirements of:

(a) the Higher National Diplomas (H.N.D.) in Hotel, Catering and Institutional Management; and

(b) the Bachelor of Arts (B.A.) and Bachelor of Science (B.Sc.) degrees awarded in Hotel, Catering and Institutional Administration.

Notable changes to this edition of Volume 2 are:

1. The comprehensive example in Chapter 2 Published Accounts of Limited Companies, formerly Chapter 3, has been re-drafted in respect of style of presentation in keeping with modern practice.

2. Chapter 5, Cost Characteristics, is an entirely new chapter and deals with the various components, groupings, behaviour and uses of costs as an aid to management decision-making.

3. Chapter 7, Budgetary Control, formerly Chapter 10, Cost Control, has been modified and also enlarged by the extension of the section on standard food costing and introduction of responsibility accounting.

   The pricing sections in the former Chapter 9 have been used as the basis of the new Chapter 9 entitled Pricing Aspects.
4. Chapter 10, previously Chapter 11, has been amended to include the Standard System of Catering Accounting.
5. Chapter 14, formerly Chapter 15, has been completely re-written and now includes the style of presentation recommended in the recent Statement of Standard Accounting Practice No. 10.
6. The questions and problems have been extensively revised and re-written.
7. The table of further reading at the end of the previous edition has been withdrawn and where appropriate, further reading lists have been included at the end of chapters.

P.J.H.

January, 1977   P.A.H.

Certain questions at the end of chapters are reprinted by kind permission of:

Hotel, Catering and Institutional Management Association
(H.C.I.M.A.)
Institute of Cost and Management Accountants   (I.C.M.A.)
Association of Certified Accountants   (A.C.C.A.)

Chapter 2 (Volume 2) contains extracts from the *Standard Systems of Hotel and Catering Accounting* published by the Hotel and Catering Economic Development Committee to whom we are grateful for being allowed to reproduce material.

We thank also the Centre for Hotel and Catering Comparisons at the University of Strathclyde for permission to reproduce the chart of ratios used in the scheme operated by them.

CONTENTS – VOLUME 2

INTRODUCTION

PRINCIPLES and practices of accounting in the industry were dealt with in Volume 1. Still only covering the routine aspects of accounting, Chapters 1–3 will, however, enable the reader to become acquainted with the more advanced aspects of accounting, dealing as they do with the preparation of final accounts of limited companies.

Chapters 4–15 concern financial planning and control in the hotel and catering industry. With an improved understanding of finance, of costs and of the likely effect on profit of their decisions, entrepreneurs and managers are able to achieve better financial results.

An attempt has been made to lead the reader, in an orderly fashion, through the avenues of monetary information which should guide him in his executive work in the industry.

Emphasis has been placed on financial planning aspects because it is felt that herein lies management's greatest opportunity to increase earning power of the business. Financial control needs to operate as a matter of routine on the twin fronts of profit and liquidity control, the one seeing that planned turnover is met and that costs do not increase unchecked, the other making certain that solvency is maintained by having cash available for paying debts as they arise.

The balance of managerial effort required in satisfying both planning and control needs is a matter of experience and judgement, generalizations being of limited value. However, common sense dictates that the larger the resources available, the more care should be taken in deciding how they should be used, hence the formal budgetary planning systems of the large hotel group.

The term 'financial management' chosen to be included in the title of this work has been defined by writers in many ways, and it is appropriate to state the interpretation used here which is that it is concerned with the policy decisions involved in the setting of a long term financial objective, and the achievement of it by the procurement, deployment and disposal of funds. Funds may for this purpose be regarded as cash. As such, financial management provides the framework within which the more routine aspects of management accounting operate.

Management accounting has been defined as 'the frequent use by management of accounting information in planning and running a business. The aim of management accounting is to interlink accounting information with the daily considerations of management so that, when decisions affecting sales, expenditure and profit are to be made, all the essential information is available in a form that can readily be understood.' This quotation is taken from *An introduction to a standard system of hotel accounting for managers of small hotels* which was developed by the Hotel and Catering Economic Development Committee.

The divisions between financial management and management accounting are blurred for they make an integrated whole in an organization; therefore no attempt has been made in this book to separate them. Further, the owner of the small establishment is concerned with and discharges both functions. Only in the very large hotel group will the distinction between the two functions be clear, but here the financial management will be at board of director level whilst the management accounting function will be at unit level.

CHAPTER ONE

ACCOUNTS OF LIMITED COMPANIES

IN the eyes of the law a company is a separate legal entity. It may enter into contracts and be sued for breach of contract. A company enjoys the advantage of perpetual succession, which means the death or withdrawal of its proprietors (shareholders) does not give cause for the company to cease trading.

Types of Companies
Companies may be formed either by:
1. Royal Charter, e.g. East India Company, or
2. Special Act of Parliament, e.g. Mersey Docks and Harbour Board
3. Registration under the Companies Act 1948 and 1967.

Kinds of Registered Companies

Unlimited Companies:
These are companies which do not afford their members (shareholders) limitation in respect of debts incurred in the cause of trading. This means that in the event of an unlimited company defaulting, then the shareholders become liable to make good such debts which have arisen.

Companies Limited by Guarantee:
Refers to companies whose members each guarantee to contribute a certain sum of money in the event of the Company being wound up. Professional bodies are among the few kinds of companies of this nature, e.g. Hotel, Catering and Institutional Management Association, Institute of Cost and Management Accountants, and so on.

Limited Companies:
These are companies which are 'limited by shares', that is to say in respect of debts or other financial crisis occurring, the liability of the shareholders is restricted (limited) to the amount of their investment (shares) in the company. This kind of company forms by far the largest number in industry and commerce today and therefore discussion and explanation is centred on the limited company.

Limited Companies

Limited companies may be divided into 'private' and 'public'. A private limited company is basically one which by virtue of its articles is restricted in the right to transfer its shares from person to person, is limited (exclusive of employees or past employees) to fifty shareholders and is legally bound not to invite the public to subscribe for any shares or debentures of the Company. From the foregone facts it may clearly be said that a public company is one which is not, in the legal sense, a private company, that is, it may transfer shares and offer shares to the public and there is no upper limit on its number of shareholders. The minimum number of shareholders allowed, by law, to form a private company is two and in the case of a public company is seven.

Below is a chart illustrating the types and kinds of companies:

Incorporation of Companies

In order to acquire incorporation both public and private companies must comply with the requirements of the Companies Act, 1948. Among the requirements both public and private companies must submit to the Registrar of Companies certain documents, the two most important being a 'Memorandum of Association' and 'Articles of Association'.

Memorandum of Association:
The Act provides that the memorandum of association of every company must state, among other things:
  (a) The name of the company, with 'limited' as the last word of the name in the case of a company limited by shares or by guarantee.
  (b) The objects of the company.
  (c) The liability of shareholders.
  (d) The amount of its share capital and the division thereof into shares of a fixed amount.

Articles of Association:
The act provides that unlimited companies and companies limited by guarantee must submit articles of association wherefore a limited company may prepare

its own articles of association but in the event of not doing so then a set of standard articles known as Table A will automatically apply to the company.

The articles of association are rules which govern the internal affairs of a company, such matters as the issue and forfeiture of shares, meeting procedure, directors' duties and responsibilities and shareholders' obligations and rights.

Preliminary or Formation Expenses:
These are expenses incurred in forming a company and include such items as legal fees for drafting the memorandum and articles of association, registration fees, stamp duties and various printing costs. These expenses are debited in a preliminary expenses account.

Capital Structure
The following list explains the terms used in connection with the capital of a limited company:

Authorized or Registered or Nominal Share Capital:
All these terms similarly mean the maximum amount of share capital, stated in a company's memorandum of association, that the company has the power to issue.

Issued or Subscribed Share Capital:
Both terms similarly mean the total nominal (face value) of shares allotted to members even though a certain number may be only partly paid.

Called-up Share Capital:
This refers to that part of the issued share capital for which cash has been requested. A company is not bound to call up all its issued share capital at once.

Paid-up Share Capital:
This refers to that part of the called-up share capital for which payment has been received.

Uncalled Share Capital:
This refers to that part of the issued share capital which has not been called up.

Unissued Share Capital:
This refers to that part of the authorized share capital which has not been allotted to members.

Shares
A share is a fixed unit of a limited company's capital. It may also be said to be a measure of an investor's interest and his liability within a company. For instance, if an individual purchases ten one-pound shares in a company then his investment is ten pounds and his liability, in the event of the company suffering financial difficulties, is limited to his ten pound investment.

Shares are divided into three classes:
Preference
Ordinary
Deferred

Preference Shares:
These normally have the first claim to a fixed non-cumulative dividend on current profits available for distribution. They also usually have prior claim of capital repayments in the case of a company winding-up.

Cumulative Preference Shares:
These are similar to preference shares with an additional advantage to the investor in the sense that dividends not paid to the holder in one year accumulate until the company can afford to pay.

Participating Preference Shares:
Again, these are similar to preference shares plus the additional benefit of participating in surplus profits (if available) after the ordinary shareholders have received a dividend.

Redeemable Preference Shares:
These may be non-cumulative, cumulative or participating. A company issuing such shares may, at a future date, redeem them, either out of profits or out of the proceeds of a fresh issue of shares. These shares may not be redeemed unless they are fully paid.

Ordinary Shares:
Dividends are paid on these shares after the preference share dividends have been met. The ordinary share capital of a company is termed 'equity' or 'risk' capital. The fortunes of these shareholders usually fluctuate with profit earned by a company, but they normally hold the voting control of a company.

Deferred or Founders' Shares:
Dividends are not declared on these shares until the entitlements of the preference and ordinary shareholders have been met. They tend, in practice, to be obtained by the promoters or founders of a company and sometimes by the vendors of a company.

Debentures
A debenture is a loan, therefore it follows that a debenture bond is a company's acknowledgement of a loan. A debenture holder is not a member (proprietor) of a company but simply a creditor, who is paid interest (normally half-yearly) which must be met even if the company sustains a loss. A shareholder (proprietor) may only receive a part dividend, in lean years, or no dividend at all.

As in the case of shares, debentures may be redeemable on or before a certain date, irredeemable or convertible. A convertible debenture is one which is issued to the public with the right (on certain terms), at a future date, to convert into ordinary shares.

Debentures may be 'naked' or 'secured'. If 'naked' then the company only undertakes to repay the loan without offering security. In the case of 'secured' (mortgage) debentures, then the company undertaking to repay a loan is secured by a charge on certain of its assets (termed a 'fixed charge') or the business as a whole (termed a 'floating charge').

Fairly frequently companies issue debentures as collateral security for bank loans and overdrafts. Collateral security is a secondary security and normally applies to the rendering of documents, e.g. debenture bonds, conveying the right to assets, e.g. cash, investments, property, etc., so that in the event of failure to settle a loan or other liability, there may be at least some benefit available to the lender without the necessity to embark on legal proceedings.

Accounting Treatment of Shares and Debentures
The manner in which shares and debentures are issued and recorded in the accounts is similar in both cases. Below are examples illustrating the issuing of shares and debentures and the effect on the balance sheet of a company.

Exhibit 1–1
Issue of Shares and Debentures – payable in full.

A company issued 40,000 6% preference shares of £1 each, 20,000 ordinary shares of £1 each and 500 7% debentures bonds of £20 each. These were all subscribed and fully paid up.

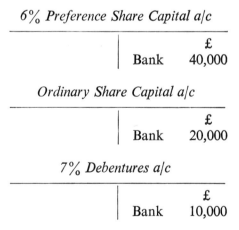

6% Preference Share Capital a/c

	£
Bank	40,000

Ordinary Share Capital a/c

	£
Bank	20,000

7% Debentures a/c

	£
Bank	10,000

Clearly double entry is completed by debiting the bank account in the cash book.

Balance Sheet

Issued Share Capital	£			£
40,000 6% preference shares				
of £1 each fully paid	40,000			
20,000 ordinary shares				
of £1 each fully paid	20,000			
Long Term Liabilities				
500 7% debentures			Cash at bank	70,000
of £20 each	10,000			
	70,000			70,000

Exhibit 1–2

Issues of shares and debentures at a premium.

A company issued 10,000 ordinary shares of £1 each at £1·20 each and 100 $7\frac{1}{2}$% debentures of £50 each at a premium of 10%. These were all subscribed and fully paid.

Ordinary Share Capital a/c

	£
Bank	10,000

Share Premium a/c

	£
Bank	2,000

$7\frac{1}{2}$% Debentures a/c

	£
Bank	5,000

Debenture Premium a/c

	£
Bank	500

Balance Sheet

Issued Share Capital	£		£
10,000 ordinary shares			
of £1 each, fully paid	10,000		
Reserves			
Share premium a/c	2,000		
Debenture premium a/c	500		
Long Term Liabilities			
100 7½% debentures			
of £50 each	5,000	Cash at bank	17,500
	17,500		17,500

Exhibit 1–3
Issue of shares and debentures at a discount.

A company issued 5,000 6½% preference shares of £1 each at £0·95 and 300 5% debentures bonds of £10 each at a discount of 6%. These were all subscribed and fully paid.

6½% Preference Share Capital a/c

		£
	Bank	4,750
	Share	
	discount a/c	250

Share Discount a/c

	£	
6½% preference		
share capital a/c	250	

5% Debentures a/c

		£
	Bank	2,820
	Debenture	
	discount a/c	180

Debenture Discount a/c

	£	
5% debenture a/c	180	

Balance Sheet

Issued Share Capital	£		£
5,000 6½% preference shares			
of £1 each fully paid	5,000		
Long Term Liabilities		Cash at bank	7,570
300 5% debentures		Share discount	250
of £10 each fully paid	3,000	Debenture discount	180
	8,000		8,000

Provisions and Reserves

The Companies Act, 1967, defines a provision as 'any amount written off or retained by way of providing for depreciation, renewal or diminution in the value of assets or retained by way of providing for any known liability of which the amount cannot be determined with substantial accuracy'. The Act does not directly define a reserve but states, in other words, that a reserve is not a provision.

The provision for depreciation, renewals, etc., is fairly straightforward and have been dealt with in Chapter 8 of Volume 1 but the second kind, i.e. for a known liability etc., is not so clear. However, company corporation tax (discussed below) is an example and the setting up of a provision for deferred repairs another.

Reserves are fundamentally divided into capital and revenue. Capital reserve examples are premiums received on issuing shares, profits set aside for redeeming shares, and so on, these being amounts which are not allowed to be used wholly or partly for distribution in the form of dividends. Revenue reserves, e.g. general reserve and balance of undistributed profits, are available, if so decided, as dividends.

To assist in deciding whether a particular item is, for legal purposes, a provision or reserve the following are considered reasonable in accounting circles:

(a) provisions are debited to the profit and loss account
(b) reserves are debited to the profit and loss appropriation account
(c) reserves are free and not intended to meet any contingencies, liabilities or losses known to exist at the date of the balance sheet.
(d) provisions may be for specific items existing at the date of the balance sheet which cannot be substantially estimated.

Corporation Tax

United Kingdom Corporation Tax is applicable to limited companies. Sole traders and partnerships remain liable to income tax. Corporation Tax is assessed on the profits[1] arising in a company's accounting period. The rate of

---

[1]Profits for corporation tax purposes comprise income and capital gains.

which is normally announced in the annual budget and relates to the previous financial year 1st April–31st March. In practice, the figure of net profit to be found in the profit and loss account is unlikely to be the amount on which corporation tax is assessable. This is because certain adjustments are usually necessary to arrive at the profit figure assessable for Corporation Tax purposes. One such adjustment is depreciation of fixed assets. Depreciation itself is not allowable for corporation tax purposes and is therefore added back to net profit. However, the Inland Revenue does make allowances for depreciation in the form of 'Capital Allowances' which may be deductible from profits.

Advance Corporation Tax (ACT)

When a company resident in the United Kingdom pays a dividend it will be liable to make an advance payment of corporation tax[2] calculated by reference to that distribution at the rate in force for the financial year in which the distribution is made. The rate of ACT for the financial year 1974 (year ended 31st March, 1975) was $33\frac{1}{3}\%$ on the gross dividend. Therefore, if a company paid a dividend on 30th June, 1974, of £1,500 it will be liable to account for ACT of $\frac{1}{3} \times £1,500 = £500$. The gross dividend plus ACT is described as a 'franked payment' which in the example is £2,000. If the recipient of a dividend is a company resident in the United Kingdom the amount of value of the dividend together with a tax credit for the ACT is known as 'franked investment income'. Such income is not liable to corporation tax by the receiving company. Subject to certain limitations, any ACT paid in respect of dividends made in an accounting period may be set-off against the corporation tax on income of that period, so reducing the total corporation tax liability.

Below is an example of how the set-off of ACT operates, so as to reduce a company's mainstream corporation tax liability.

Exhibit 1–4

In the year to 31st March, 1975, a company has a profit assessable for corporation tax of £100,000 and pay dividends of £30,000 in that year. Assume a corporation tax rate of 50% and an ACT rate of $33\frac{1}{3}\%$.

		£	£
ACT	£30,000 × $33\frac{1}{3}\%$		10,000
Corporation tax liability	£100,000 × 50%	50,000	
Less: ACT		10,000	
Mainstream corporation tax payable at due date:			40,000
Total corporation tax paid:			50,000

The shareholders resident ir the United Kingdom receive £30,000 together with a tax credit of £10,000.

[2]For further reading on advance corporation tax, refer to the end of this chapter.

Accounting Treatment of Corporation Tax

Below, Exhibit 1–5 illustrates how corporation tax[3] may be treated in the accounts of limited companies:

Exhibit 1–5

A limited company prepares its annual accounts on 31st December. For the year ended 31st December, 1974, its liability for corporation tax on that year's profits was estimated at £10,250. On 30th September, 1975, the corporation tax liability on the previous year's profits was agreed at £10,100. The corporation tax liability in respect of profits for the year ended 31st December, 1975, was estimated to be at £12,500. Corporation tax for the previous year's profits is payable on 1st January each year. All tax payments were made on the due dates.

Corporation Tax a/c

1974		£	1974		£
Dec. 31	Balance c/d	10,250	Dec. 31	Profit and Loss a/c	10,250
		10,250			10,250
1975			1975		
Dec. 31	Profit and Loss a/c	150	Jan. 1	Balance b/d	10,250
	Balance b/d	22,600	Dec. 31	Profit and Loss a/c	12,500
		22,750			22,750
1976			1976		
Jan. 1	Bank	10,100	Jan. 1	Balance b/d	10,100
					12,500

Profit and Loss Account (*extract*) for year ended 31st Dec. 1974

Corporation Tax	£10,250	

Balance Sheet (*extract*) 31st Dec. 1974

	£
Provision for Corporation Tax	10,250

Profit and Loss Account (*extract*) for year ended 31st Dec., 1975

Corporation Tax	£12,500	Over Provision of tax £150

Balance Sheet (*extract*) 31st Dec., 1975

	£
Provision for Corporation Tax	12,500
Current liabilities	
Corporation Tax	10,100

[3]For the sake of simplicity ACT has been completely ignored in respect of this and all other limited company accounts examples.

It may be seen in Exhibit 1–5 above, that the amount of corporation tax payable at the end of a period is estimated and charged to that period. The following year when the figure is agreed by the Inland Revenue then an adjustment is effected in that year, i.e. an overprovision being a credit (increasing net profit) in the profit and loss account, as in the above case, and an underprovision being debited (decreasing net profit) therein. The balance sheet extracts illustrate that a current year's corporation tax estimate (after adjustment) is shown as a current liability.

Profit and Loss Appropriation Account

Fundamentally, the profit and loss appropriation account of a limited company is where net profit, after providing for taxation is divided.

To net profit after tax is added the balance of the previous year's unappropriated profits (if a credit balance) and any over-provision of taxation attributable thereto. The various appropriations are then deducted from the resulting figure. These include transfers to reserves[4] and any dividends whether proposed or already paid. The balance is carried forward to the next year. This balance is listed under reserves in the balance sheet.

Exhibit 1–6

An example of a company's profit and loss account is illustrated in vertical form, below:

Profit and Loss Appropriation Account
for year ended 31st December, 1976

	£	£
NET PROFITS after tax		70,000
Unappropriated profit		
b/f from previous year	7,700	
Overprovision of tax from		
previous year	300	8,000
Less: Appropriations		
10% Debenture redemption		
reserve fund	6,000	
General reserve	9,000	
Dividends (Gross):		
Paid: 8% Preference share	8,000	
Ordinary Share (4%)	16,000	
Proposed:		
Ordinary Share (6%)	24,000	
		63,000
Unappropriated profits c/f to next year		15,000

[4]Examples being preference share or debenture redemption reserve (sinking) fund and general reserve.

Balance Sheet

Having considered the capital, reserve and loan structures of limited companies it is important to observe the order in which they, and their component parts, are arranged on a balance sheet.

Exhibit 1–7

Illustrated below in vertical form is an example of a limited company balance sheet:

Balance Sheet as at 31st December, 1976

Fixed Assets	Cost £	Depr. £	Net £
Freehold premises	569,000	—	569,000
Furniture and equipment	103,500	30,000	73,500
	672,500	30,000	642,500

Current Assets			
Stocks	34,000		
Debtors	29,000		
Bank and cash	9,500		
		72,500	

Less: Current Liabilities			
Creditors	13,000		
Corporation Tax (on previous year's profits)	30,000		
Proposed dividends: 6% on ordinary shares	24,000		
		67,000	

Working Capital			5,500
Capital Employed			648,000

FINANCED BY:

Share Capital	Auth. £	Issued £
100,000 8% Preference shares of £1 each, fully paid	100,000	100,000
400,000 Ordinary shares of £1 each, fully paid	400,000	400,000
	500,000	500,000

Reserves

Share premium	10,000	
10% debenture redemption reserve fund	6,000	
General reserve	62,000	
Unappropriated profit c/f	15,000	
	———	93,000
SHAREHOLDERS FUNDS/INVESTMENT		593,000
10% Debentures	20,000	
Future Corporation Tax (on current year's profits)	35,000	55,000
	———	———
		648,000

It will be observed that the paid dividends do not appear in the balance sheet as the liability to pay has been discharged by the payment itself.

Questions and Problems

1–1 What do you understand by 'the principle of limited liability'?

1–2 Describe the difference between the capital structure of a sole trader and a limited company.

1–3 How is it possible that the authorized and issued share capital of one company may be the same amount whereas in another company there may be a considerable disparity between the two?

1–4 Compare and contrast shares and debentures.

1–5 An hotel company transacted the following:
(a) 15,000 ordinary shares of £1 each at a premium of £0·15; and
(b) 5,000 9% debentures of £5 each at a discount of £0·20.
Show the appropriate extracts in the company's balance sheet.

1–6 Smart Service Co. Ltd. has an authorized share capital of £150,000 comprising 50,000 preference shares of £1 each issued and fully paid and £100,000 ordinary shares of £1 each of which 50,000 are issued and fully paid.
The details below relate to the company on 31st January 1977:

	£
General Reserve	12,000
Current Assets	28,000
Current liabilities	22,000
Fixed Assets	190,000
Unappropriated profit	10,000
Provision for depreciation on fixed assets	20,000
11% Debenture	54,000

Draft a summarized balance sheet for the company as at 31st January, 1977, indicating shareholders' funds, working capital and capital employed.

1-7   The following trial balance was extracted from the records of Fishers Restaurants Ltd. as at 28th February, 1977:

	£'000	£'000
Authorized and issued share capital:		
500,000 ordinary shares of £1 each		500
Directors' remuneration	50	
Retained profit b/f 29th February, 1976		17
Debtors and creditors	22	26
Wages and salaries	110	
Provision for depreciation on equipment		
to 29th February, 1976		5
Equipment, at cost	24	
Freehold land and buildings, at cost	510	
Stocks of food and beverages	13	
Repairs and renovations	7	
Purchases and sales	180	420
Administration	10	
Laundry	4	
Rates and insurances	12	
Cash in hand	3	
Balance at bank	25	
Advance booking deposits		2
	970	970

The following information is relevant:
(a) Stocks of food and beverages at 28.2.77, £16,000
(b) Provision for depreciation on equipment is to be made at the rate of 10% per annum using the straight line method.
(c) Rates and insurances paid in advance at 31.2.77, £4,000.
(d) Provide for a dividend of 10%.
You are required to prepare a trading, profit and loss account for the year ended 28th February, 1977, and a balance sheet as at that date.

1-8   The Midville Catering Company commenced business on 1st April, 1975. Its authorized capital was 50,000 ordinary shares of £1 each and 50,000 5% preference shares of £1 each. The company has issued 50,000 of each class of share and these are fully paid up. From the following trial balance extracted from the books of the company after the preparation of the trading account, you are required to prepare a profit and loss account for the year ended 31st March, 1977, and a balance sheet as at that date.

	£	£
Ordinary share capital		50,000
5% preference share capital		50,000
6% debentures		20,000
Share premium account		5,000
Gross profit		35,405
Directors' fees	3,000	
Auditors' fees	500	
Administrative expenses	10,000	
Selling expenses	4,000	
Other expenses	2,000	
6% Debenture interest (6 months)	600	
Preliminary expenses	1,800	
Discounts received		450
Dividends received		200
Discounts allowed	150	
Sundry debtors	4,500	
Sundry creditors		6,000
Cash at banks	3,655	
Stock in trade	9,000	
Fixed assets, at cost		
Catering premises	87,600	
Furnishings	22,000	
Equipment	12,000	
Linen	6,500	
Advanced booking deposit		250
	167,305	167,305

Take into account the following adjustments:
1. Depreciate all fixed assets, except premises at 10% per annum on cost.
2. Accrued administration expenses are £80.
3. Prepaid other expenses are £75.
4. Provide £450 against bad debts.
5. Provide £4,000 for corporation tax, payable 1st January, 1977.
6. Provide for a dividend of 5% on ordinary shares.
7. Transfer £1,500 to general reserve.
8. Allow for a further 6 months' debenture interest.

Further Reading
1. *Corporation Tax* (I.R.18) Inland Revenue, H.M.S.O.
2. Wood, F., *Business Accounting* (Vol II) Longmans; Chapters 34 to 42.
3. Williams, R. G., *Comprehensive Aspects of Taxation* (Revised by B. Mendes), Donnington Press.

CHAPTER TWO

PUBLISHED ACCOUNTS OF LIMITED COMPANIES

A T the end of its financial year a company is required, under the Companies Act, 1948, to submit a profit and loss account and balance sheet, directors' report and an auditor's report. One of each of these three documents must be sent to each shareholder and debenture holder and filed with the Registrar of Companies.

The Companies Acts, 1948 and 1967, require a considerable amount of disclosures to be made in the annual accounts and directors' report. Perhaps the most important provision is contained in Section 149 of the 1948 Act which states that every profit and loss account of a company shall give a true and fair view of the profit or loss of the company for the financial year, and every balance sheet of a company shall give a true and fair view of the state of the affairs of the company as at the end of its financial year.

Published Profit and Loss Account

Disclosures, other than net profit before and after tax and appropriations, may either be compiled within the body of the profit and loss account or in the form of notes within the directors' report.

The more important disclosures required by the Acts are summarized below:

(a) Turnover: must be stated if it exceeds £50,000.
(b) Investment Income; this must be separated into
   (i) quoted investment income, and
   (ii) unquoted investment income
(c) Directors' Remuneration; the aggregate totals must be shown for each of the following:
   (i) directors' emoluments, i.e. fees, salaries, etc.
   (ii) directors' or past directors' pensions
   (iii) compensation to directors' or past directors' loss of office.
(d) Loan Interest; this must be divided into:
   (i) bank loans and overdrafts, and other loans (including debentures), repayable (wholly) in five years, and
   (ii) other loans having a period of repayment exceeding five years.
(e) Hire of Plant and Machinery; this must be stated if material (this does not include hire-purchase payments).

(*f*) Provision for Depreciation; renewal or diminution of fixed assets; this must be shown and is usually divided into particular asset classes.

(*g*) Taxation; the charge for UK Corporation Tax and the basis under which the charge was computed.

(*h*) Amounts provided for the redemption of share capital or loans. Share capital means redeemable preference shares and loans indicate debentures, etc.

(*i*) Dividends; this means aggregate dividends paid and proposed.

(*j*) Provisions; amounts set aside (other than for depreciation, etc.) if material.

(*k*) Auditors' Remuneration; this includes fees and expenses.

(*l*) Reserves; this includes transfers to and from reserves, if material.

(*m*) Unappropriated profit or loss from the previous year; this is the balance, on the previous year's profit and loss account, brought forward.

(*n*) Comparative Figures; that is, the corresponding profit and loss account figures from the previous year must appear.

Published Balance Sheet

The more important disclosures apparent within the Acts are summarized as follows:

(*a*) Balance sheet items must be classified under the following groupings
- (*i*) Authorized share capital
- (*ii*) Issued share capital
- (*iii*) Reserves ⎫ Appropriate to
- (*iv*) Provisions (except depreciation, etc.) ⎬ the Company's
- (*v*) Liabilities ⎭ business.
- (*vi*) Fixed Assets
- (*vii*) Current Assets
- (*viii*) Assets which are neither fixed nor current.

(*b*) Reserves; the total amount of reserves must be shown and the following reserves must be shown separately:
- (*i*) Share premium account
- (*ii*) Capital redemption reserves fund, i.e. preference shares not debentures.

(*c*) Provisions; any items coming into the definition of provisions. Corporation Tax and amounts set aside for equalizing taxation charges, if material, must be shown separately.

(*d*) Liabilities: include debentures, bank loans and overdrafts, proposed dividends, creditors and accruals, etc.

(*e*) Fixed Assets; the following should be disclosed:
- (*i*) Aggregate cost and/or valuation of the assets
- (*ii*) Aggregate depreciation/amortization written off
- (*iii*) Value of land and buildings distinguishing freehold long lease (50 years or over) and short lease (under 50 years).
- (*vi*) Goodwill, patents and trade-marks, less amounts written off.

(*f*) Current Assets; if the realizable value is lower than the book value this must be stated.

(*g*) Investments; quoted investments must be shown at cost and market value at the date of the balance sheet. Unquoted investments must be shown at cost and directors' estimated valuation at the date of the balance sheet.

(*h*) Capital Expenditure; the total amount of contracts placed for capital expenditure for which no provision in the accounts has been made, plus the estimated capital expenditure authorized by the directors, not yet contracted for, must be stated.

(*i*) Comparative Figures; as in the case of the profit and loss account, the corresponding balance sheet figures from the previous year must appear.

General Legal Points
Share Premium Account:
It has already been mentioned that when shares are issued at a premium, the premium must be transferred to a share premium account.

A share premium balance (if any) may be used in the following circumstances only:

(*a*) the issue of fully paid bonus shares providing the company has not issued all its authorized capital

(*b*) to write off:
    (*i*) preliminary expenses
    (*ii*) discounts, expenses and commissions incurred in the issue of shares or debentures

(*c*) in the case of the redemption of shares or debentures at a premium, then the premium payable on redemption may be provided out of share premium.

Note: Preliminary expenses may also be written off in the profit and loss appropriation account.

Comprehensive Example
Exhibit 2–1
Circle Hotels Limited have an authorized share capital of £800,000, consisting of 600,000 shares of £1 each, and 200,000 8% cumulative preference shares of £1 each.

The balances in the books at 31st December, 1976, are as below:

	£	£
Ordinary shares issued		590,000
Preference shares issued		150,000
Share premium		10,000
Unquoted investments at cost	70,000	
Quoted investments at cost (market value £81,000)	90,000	
Freehold land at cost	400,000	
Freehold buildings at cost	230,000	
Leasehold buildings on long lease	120,000	
Leasehold buildings on short lease	54,600	
Plant and machinery at cost	187,000	
Furniture and fittings at cost	93,000	
Depreciation to 31st December, 1975:		
Freehold buildings		35,000
Plant and machinery		93,000
Furniture and fittings		9,300
Amortization to 31st December, 1975:		
Long lease		10,000
Short lease		4,600
9% debentures 1983/88, secured on freehold buildings		160,000
General reserve		63,000
Unappropriated profits, for year ended 31st December, 1975		16,000
Corporation Tax, year to 31st December, 1975		79,000
Bank Overdraft		64,000
Creditors		105,700
9% debenture redemption sinking fund		15,000
Provision for doubtful debts		3,300
Stock at or under cost, 1st January 1976	75,100	
Hire of equipment	1,300	
Debtors	276,700	
Cash in hand	15,500	
Debenture interest (gross) for year to 31st December, 1976	14,400	
Income from unquoted investments (gross)		8,700
Income from quoted investments (gross)		6,900
Sales (net)		1,823,200
Purchase of food, liquor, etc.	862,600	
Wages and salaries	273,800	
Operating expenses	470,700	
Preference dividend to 31st December, 1976	12,000	
	3,246,700	3,246,700

The following information is relevant:

1. Capital expenditure; the company has entered into contracts worth £142,000 and authorized £40,000. Neither amounts have been provided for in the accounts.
2. Provision for doubtful debts is to be increased to £5,200.
3. Depreciation and amortization for the year to 31st December, 1976, is as follows:

	£
freehold buildings	4,200
leasehold buildings – long lease	10,000
leasehold buildings – short lease	4,600
plant and machinery	16,700
furniture and fittings	3,900

4. Directors' remuneration of £5,000 fees and £12,000 salaries is to be provided for in the accounts.
5. Provide in the accounts for auditors' remuneration of £4,000.
6. A professional valuation of the company's freehold land was carried out on 31st December, 1976, with a resulting valuation of £625,000, and the directors decided to bring the new value into the balance sheet.
7. Corporation Tax liability for the year ended 31st December, 1976, has now been agreed at £86,000. The estimated corporation tax on the current year's profits is £68,000, based on 50% of assessable profits for the year.
8. The directors decided to pay an ordinary dividend for the year of 11% on 27th March, 1977.
9. Stock on 31st December, 1976, at or under cost is £93,700.
10. It has been decided to transfer £10,000 to the general reserve and £15,000 to the 9% debenture redemption sinking fund.
11. Directors' valuation of the unquoted investment is £75,000.

From the above information, the following documents may be prepared, bearing in mind the Companies Act (as far as possible) in a form suitable for publication and presentation to shareholders at the company's annual general meeting:

(a) a profit and loss account for the year ended 31st December, 1976, and
(b) a balance sheet as at that date.

CIRCLE HOTELS LIMITED

Profit and Loss Account for the year ended 31st December, 1976

Notes	1976		1975	
	£	£	£	£
Turnover for the year		1,823,200		1,560,800
1. Net Profit before Taxation		172,300		162,500
Less: U.K. Corporation Tax		68,000		79,000
2. Net profit after Taxation		104,300		83,600
Less: Appropriations				
Transfer to 9% debenture redemption sinking fund	15,000		15,000	
Transfer to general reserve	10,000		10,000	
8% preference dividend— paid 31.12.76	12,000		12,000	
Proposed ordinary divident of 11%— payable 27.3.77	64,900	101,900	31,100	68,100
		2,400		15,500
3. *Add:* Unappropriated profit from previous year brought forward		9,000		500
Unappropriated profits carried forward to next year		11,400		16,000

Notes to the profit and loss account:

1. Net profit before taxation was arrived at
   (*a*) after charging:

	1976	1975
	£	£
(*i*) Loan interest on 9% debentures	14,400	14,400
(*ii*) Amortization and depreciation :		
Freehold buildings	4,200	4,200
Leasehold buildings – long lease	10,000	10,000
Leasehold buildings – short lease	4,600	4,600
Plant and machinery	16,700	14,000
Furniture and fittings	3,900	3,500
(*iii*) Directors' emoluments	17,000	12,500
Auditors' remuneration	4,000	3,800
Hire of equipment	1,300	3,900

	1976 £	1975 £
(b) after adding income from:		
(i) Quoted investments	6,900	6,800
(ii) Unquoted investments	8,700	8,400

2. Corporation tax is based on assessable profits for the year at a rate of 50%

	1976	1975
3. Unappropriated profit brought forward	16,000	2,000
Underprovision of taxation (deduct)	7,000	1,500

CIRCLE HOTELS LIMITED

Balance Sheet as at 31st December, 1976

Notes	1976 £	£	1975 £	£
1. FIXED ASSETS		1,118,300		934,700
2. INVESTMENTS		175,000		160,000
3. CURRENT ASSETS				
Stocks	93,700		75,100	
Debtors, less provision	256,500		150,400	
Cash in hand	15,500	365,700	11,300	236,800
Less: CURRENT LIABILITIES				
Creditors and accruals	126,700		160,500	
Corporation tax – previous year's profits	86,000		79,000	
Bank overdrafts	64,000		118,000	
Proposed dividends	64,900	(341,600)	31,000	(388,500)
		1,317,400		943,000
FINANCED BY:		£		£
4. SHARE CAPITAL		740,000		600,000
5. RESERVES		349,400		104,000
Shareholders Interest/Investment		1,089,400		704,000
6. LOAN CAPITAL		160,000		160,000
Corporation Tax – current year's profits		68,000		79,000
		1,317,400		943,000

Arthur Wain, *Chairman*   Rex Bonnington, *Managing Director*

Notes to the balance sheet:

1. Fixed Assets:

	Cost or Valuation £	1976 Amort or Depn. £	Net Book Value £	Cost or Valuation £	1975 Amort and Depn. £	Net Book Value £
Freehold land	625,000	—	625,000	400,000	—	400,000
Freehold buildings	230,000	39,200	190,800	230,000	35,000	195,000
Leasehold buildings – long lease	120,000	20,000	100,000	120,000	10,000	110,000
Leasehold buildings – short lease	54,600	9,200	45,400	54,600	4,600	50,000
Plant and machinery	187,000	109,700	77,300	189,000	93,000	96,000
Furniture and fittings	93,000	13,200	79,800	93,000	9,300	83,700
	1,309,600	191,300	1,118,300	1,086,600	151,900	934,700

2. Investments:

	1976 £	1975 £
Quoted (Market value £81,000; 1975 £85,000)	105,000	90,000
Unquoted (Directors' valuation £75,000; 1975 £72,000)	70,000	70,000
	175,000	160,000

3. Stocks have been valued at the lower of cost and net realizable value.

4. Share Capital: 1975 and 1976

	Authorized £	Issued £
8% preference shares of £1 each fully paid	200,000	150,000
Ordinary shares of £1 each fully paid	600,000	590,000
	800,000	740,000

5. Reserves:

	1976 £	1975 £
Share premium account	10,000	10,000
Fixed asset revaluation reserve	225,000	—
9% debenture redemption sinking fund	30,000	15,000
General reserve	73,000	63,000
Unappropriated profits carried forward to next year	11,400	16,000
	349,400	104,000

6. Loan Capital:
   9% debentures 1983/88 (secured on freehold buildings)

1976 £	1975 £
160,000	160,000

7. Capital expenditure:

	1976 £	1975 £
Authorized	40,000	55,000
Committed	142,000	—
	182,000	55,000

The points enumerated below are offered to assist the reader in understanding the construction of the above annual published accounts in Exhibit 2–1.

(a) The comparative figures used in the example are not detailed in the initial question information but have been included by reason of completing a more practical picture.

(*b*) The net operating profit after charging legal disclosures was calculated as:

	£	£
Sales (net)		1,823,200
Less: Cost of goods sold		
Stocks (1st January, 1976)	75,100	
Add: Purchases of food, liquor, etc.	862,600	
	937,700	
Less: Stocks (31st December, 1976)	93,700	
		844,000
GROSS PROFIT		979,200
Less: Overheads (that are not required to be disclosed)		
Provision for doubtful debts increase	1,900	
Wages and salaries	273,800	
Operating expenses	470,700	
		746,400
PROFIT (before charging the legal disclosures)		232,800
Less: Other Overheads		
9% debenture interest	14,400	
Amortization and depreciation	39,400	
Directors' remuneration	17,000	
Auditors' remuneration	4,000	
Hire of equipment	1,300	
		76,100
PROFIT (after charging legal disclosures)		156,700

(*c*) The under provision of Corporation Tax is calculated by subtracting the agreed tax (£86,000) from the previous year's estimated tax (£79,000), the result, i.e. £7,000, is adjusted on the unappropriated profits brought forward as this is the profit concerned.

(*d*) Notice both the paid and proposed dividends appear in the profit and loss appropriation account but in the balance sheet only the proposed dividend appears (as a current liability). The reason for this difference is that both are appropriations therefore appear in profit and loss but as the preference dividend has been paid only the proposed ordinary dividend remains a liability.

(*e*) The appreciation on valuation of the company's freehold land (£225,000) is effected in the books (and so on the balance sheet) by increasing (debiting) the freehold land and opening a capital reserve account, i.e. fixed asset revaluation reserve, and crediting the amount therein. As this class of reserve is not strictly required to be disclosed the £225,000 and other similar reserves may be grouped together in the balance sheet under the heading of capital reserves.

(*f*) Again, although not within the context of the example information, it will be observed that the difference between the quoted investments of 1975 and 1976 (£15,000) would in effect represent the amount of cash invested in securities thus complementing the annual instalment of profit transferred to the debenture redemption sinking fund.

Finally, it is important to be aware that the Companies Acts do not stipulate a particular style of presenting published accounts, but only lay down requirements concerning disclosure of information. It will be frequently observed in published accounts that a great deal of the information is within the attached notes whilst the accounts themselves merely house the financial framework of a company, the reason being that excessive detail required by the Acts would cause the annual accounts to become unwieldy.

Directors' Report
This document, along with the notes on the published accounts, must be attached to the balance sheet. The report does not form part of the published accounts but in brief contains the following information:

1. Proposed dividends and transfers to or from reserves.
2. The directors' interests in the company, i.e. any shares or debentures they may own.
3. Any political or charitable donations where they total more than £50.
4. Particulars of significant contracts (if at all) in which the directors have or had material interests.
5. The principal activities of the company and any major changes therein.
6. The average number of employees employed each week and the aggregate total of remuneration due to them. This only applies where the average exceeds 100 employees.
7. The market value of freehold and leasehold lands and buildings if they differ materially from the balance sheet values.

Auditors' Report
This report basically informs the shareholders and other interested parties that the profit and loss account and balance sheet, and the notes pertaining to them, give a true and fair view of the company's profit (or loss) for that year ended and the company's affairs as at that date and comply with the Companies Acts, 1948, 1967. In normal circumstances the actual details of an auditors' report is not required to be disclosed to members, etc., but are retained by the directors for any action to be taken thereon.

Questions and Problems
2–1 Describe, as if to a layman, the main differences between 'published' and 'internal' annual accounts as prepared by a limited liability company.

2–2 The following statement was made by an irate shareholder of a limited liability company. 'It is seemingly absurd that directors and management who are only employees have full access to the annual figures of a limited company whereas we, the shareholders, who are the owners receive only certain disclosures, laid down by law.' Discuss.

2–3 Westminster Hotels Ltd., which has an authorized capital of £700,000 divided into 500,000 ordinary shares of £1 each and 200,000 12% preference shares of £1 each, makes up its accounts on 30th June each year. Its trial balance at 30th June, 1976, was as follows:

	£	£
Issued and fully paid-up capital:		
Ordinary shares		350,000
Preference shares		150,000
Profit and loss account balance 1.7.75		40,000
General reserve		90,000
Freehold land and buildings, at cost	720,000	
Unquoted investment, at cost		
(Directors valuation £70,000)	55,000	
Quoted investment, at cost		
(Market value £30,000)	33,400	
Equipment at cost	75,000	
Provision for depreciation on		
equipment 1.7.75		50,000
Stock 30.6.76, at cost or net realizable		
value whichever lower	30,000	
Debtors and creditors	140,000	110,000
Balance of cash at bank and in hand	48,500	
Profit for year ended 30.6.76 subject to		
the adjustments noted below		280,000
Preference dividend for half year – paid 1.1.76	9,000	
Interim dividend of 5% on ordinary		
shares – paid 1.3.76	17,500	
Income from investments:		
Unquoted		5,400
Quoted		3,000
Corporation tax payable on previous		
year's profits		50,000
	1,128,400	1,128,400

Notes and adjustments:
1. The profit for the year ended 30th June, 1976, has been arrived at after charging £1,500 for audit fee, managing director's salary £8,000 but before charging depreciation and directors' fees which should be provided for as follows:
    (*a*) Depreciation of equipment for the year at 20% of cost; and

    (*b*) Directors fees as below:
        — Chairman £2,000
        — Three other directors including the managing director £1,000 each.

2. Corporation Tax based on assessable profits for the year at 50% is estimated at £100,000 and this should be provided for.

3. The directors recommend:
    (*a*) Payment of a preference dividend for six months on 1.7.76
    (*b*) A final dividend of 10% on the ordinary shares
    (*c*) Transfer of £80,000 to general reserve.

4. The turnover of the company for the year was £1,800,000.

You are required to prepare the profit and loss account for the year ended 30th June, 1976, and a balance sheet as at that date in a form suitable for circulation to members and to conform, as far as the information given will permit, with the requirements of the Companies Acts 1948 and 1967.

Further Reading
1. Recent published accounts of limited companies will prove useful in appreciating legal disclosures and general style of presentation.

CHAPTER THREE

CONSOLIDATED ACCOUNTS OF
LIMITED COMPANIES

SINCE so many public companies in the hotel and catering industry produce a group balance sheet and profit and loss account in addition to the usual company final accounts, some understanding is required of the reasons why and how group final accounts are prepared.

A company taking over control of another company by the purchase of shares giving majority votes, becomes a holding company of the one bought, which itself becomes a subsidiary.

The Companies Act, 1948, states it officially in Section 154:

'(1) . . . a company shall . . . be deemed to be a subsidiary of another if, but only if –
   (*a*) that other either
        (*i*) is a member of it and controls the composition of its board of directors; or
        (*ii*) holds more than half in nominal value of its equity share capital; or
   (*b*) the first mentioned company is a subsidiary of any company which is that other's subsidiary.'

A holding company with its subsidiaries is known as a group of companies, giving rise to the term 'group accounts'.

Group Accounts

Section 150 of the 1948 Companies Act requires the preparation of group accounts where a company has a subsidiary at the end of its financial year and is not a wholly-owned subsidiary of another company incorporated in Great Britain.

Section 151 of the 1948 Companies Act states among other things:

'. . . the group accounts, shall be consolidated accounts comprising:
   (*a*) a consolidated balance sheet dealing with the state of affairs of the company and all the subsidiaries to be dealt with in group accounts.
   (*b*) a consolidated profit and loss account dealing with the profit or loss of the company and those subsidiaries.'

Some other parts of Section 151 deal with exceptions to the above requirements but are beyond the scope of this book.

Preparation of Consolidated Balance Sheets

Whilst the consolidation of final accounts in practice is likely to be the work of an accountant, and may be complicated when subsidiaries hold control themselves of subsidiaries, a simple approach will suffice to enable published group accounts to be understood.

Certain rules are necessary to consolidate balance sheets, starting with the rule that the balance sheets of the holding company and its subsidiary are added together and any inter-company balances eliminated.

In all four examples which follow the balance sheet of the holding company 'H' remains unchanged, whilst four different subsidiaries are used, S(A), S(B), S(C), S(D).

Exhibit 3–1

When all shares in subsidiary are bought at nominal value and an inter-company loan exists.

Balance Sheet of 'H' Co. Ltd. on 31st December, 1976

	£		£
Issued ordinary share capital	100,000	Fixed assets	55,000
Current liabilities	10,000	Investment in S(A)	40,000
		Loan to S(A)	3,000
		Current assets	12,000
	110,000		110,000

Balance Sheet of S(A) Co. Ltd. on 31st December, 1976

	£		£
Issued ordinary share capital	40,000	Fixed assets	42,000
Loan from 'H'	3,000	Current assets	7,000
Current liabilities	6,000		
	49,000		49,000

The investment of £40,000 and loan of £3,000 are eliminated in the consolidated balance sheet; all other items are added together.

Consolidated Balance Sheet of 'H' Co. Ltd. and its
subsidiary S(A) Co. Ltd. on 31st December, 1976

	£		£
Issued ordinary share capital	100,000	Fixed assets	97,000
Current liabilities	16,000	Current assets	19,000
	116,000		116,000

The above consolidated balance sheet is in summary form only for the sake of simplicity, but reference should be made also to the following which illustrates, with sample details, how the balance sheets are combined to form the consolidated balance sheet.

*Consolidated Balance Sheet of 'H' Co. Ltd. and its
Subsidiary S(A) Co. Ltd. on 31st December, 1976*

	H £	S(A) £	H and £	S(A) £
FIXED ASSETS				
Property	45,000	35,000		80,000
Equipment	10,000	7,000		17,000
	55,000	42,000		97,000
CURRENT ASSETS				
Stocks	8,000	5,000	13,000	
Debtors	3,000	1,500	4,500	
Cash and bank	1,000	500	1,500	
	12,000	7,000	19,000	
Less: CURRENT LIABILITIES				
Taxation	2,000	1,000	3,000	
Creditors	3,000	2,000	5,000	
Overdraft	5,000	3,000	8,000	
	10,000	6,000	16,000	

NET CURRENT ASSETS (Working Capital) £19,000 − £16,000 =	3,000
NET ASSETS (Capital Employed)	100,000
SHARE CAPITAL	
100,000 ordinary shares of £1 issued and fully paid up	£100,000

Goodwill on Consolidation

Exhibit 3–2
When purchase price is greater than the value of net assets, and all shares in subsidiary are acquired.

If the cost of acquiring control of a subsidiary is in excess of its net asset value then the difference is regarded as goodwill when consolidating. Net asset value is the total assets less liabilities to outsiders.

Instead of S(A) Co. Ltd. let S(B) Co. Ltd. be acquired:

Balance Sheet of S(B) Co. Ltd. on 31st December, 1976

	£		£
Issued ordinary share capital	20,000	Fixed assets	29,000
Revenue reserves	8,000		
Profit and loss account	2,000	Current assets	7,000
(Net asset value)	30,000		
Loan from 'H'	3,000		
Current liabilities	3,000		
	36,000		36,000

'H' Co. Ltd. paid £40,000 for S(B) Co. Ltd.'s net assets worth £30,000 leaving a figure of £10,000 representing goodwill on purchase. Net assets may be calculated as shown in the balance sheet of S(B) Co. Ltd. by the addition of issued share capital and reserves, or by taking total assets (£36,000) less any liabilities to outside interests (£6,000).

The resulting consolidated balance sheet is as follows:

*Consolidated Balance Sheet of 'H' Co. Ltd.
with S(B) Co. Ltd. on 31st December, 1976*

	£		£
Issued ordinary share capital	100,000	Fixed assets	84,000
Current liabilities	13,000	Goodwill on Consolidation	
		(£40,000 – £30,000)	10,000
		Current assets	19,000
	113,000		113,000

Goodwill is dealt with in more detail in Chapter 13. Should the price paid for a subsidiary be less than its net asset value, then a capital reserve arises on consolidation.

Minority Interests on Consolidation

Exhibit 3–3
When not all shares in the subsidiary are acquired, but enough to gain control, minority interests result.

A controlling interest in a company is achieved when over 50% of the ordinary shares are acquired, assuming each share carries one vote and other shares are non-voting. If between 50% and 100% of the shares in a subsidiary are acquired, those not acquired are called the Minority Interest, and the value of these attributed to shareholders outside the group must be calculated.

The rule in this situation is that the claims of the minority shareholders must be deducted from the net asset value before calculating the value of the holding company's interest and goodwill. Preference shares, because of limited voting rights, need not be acquired and are normally taken at nominal value.

Consolidation is therefore effected by calculating net assets and deducting nominal value of preference shares. The resulting figure represents the value of equity which is then proportioned according to holding company and minority shareholdings. The consolidated balance sheet is prepared as though 100% control had been achieved, as exhibits 1 and 2, but the value of minority interests shown as a liability.

'H' Co. Ltd. bought for £40,000, 30,000 ordinary shares in S(C) Co. Ltd. whose balance sheet is as follows:

Balance Sheet of S(C) Co. Ltd. on 31st December, 1976

	£		£
Issued preference shares	20,000	Fixed assets	79,000
Issued ordinary shares of £1	50,000	Current assets	7,000
Revenue reserves	8,000		
Profit and Loss account	2,000		
	80,000		
Loan from 'H'	3,000		
Current liabilities	3,000		
	86,000		86,000

	£
Net assets: £86,000 − £6,000	80,000
Preference shareholders' claim	20,000
Value of equity	60,000

'H' Co. Ltd. bought 30,000 shares being valued at

$$\frac{30,000}{50,000} \text{ i.e. } 60\% \text{ of } £60,000 \qquad £36,000$$

Since payment of £40,000 is £4,000 more than the value of 30,000 shares, goodwill results.

Minority Interest (including preference shareholders) is

£80,000 − £36,000 £44,000

The consolidated balance sheet will appear as follows:

Consolidated Balance Sheet of 'H' Co. Ltd. and S(C) Co. Ltd.
on 31st December, 1976

	£		£
Issued ordinary shares	100,000	Fixed assets	134,000
Minority interest	44,000	Goodwill	4,000
Current liabilities	13,000	Current assets	19,000
	157,000		157,000

Pre-acquisition profits

Exhibit 3–4

Consolidating at a date after the purchase of a subsidiary gives rise to pre-acquisition and post-acquisition profits.

It has so far been assumed that the consolidated balance sheet was prepared at the time of the subsidiary's acquisition. Profits made by the subsidiary were taken into account in determining net assets and consequently goodwill or capital reserve on purchase. Pre-acquisition profits (undistributed) of subsidiary have therefore been capitalized and are not available for distribution. If not all shares are purchased, then it has been shown that only the part of the profits belonging to the holding is capitalized, the remainder being part of minority interests.

If consolidated final accounts are prepared at the end of the financial year following acquisition, it is likely that the subsidiary will have made further profits. These profits made subsequent to acquisition are available for distribution.

Clearly, then, consolidating some time after an acquisition the subsidiary's profit and loss account must be separated into

(*a*) pre-acquisition profit

(*b*) post-acquisition profit

On 30th September 1976 'H' Co. Ltd. bought for £40,000 60% (30,000) of the £1 ordinary shares of S(D) Co. Ltd. whose balance sheet on 31st December, 1976, was:

Balance Sheet of S(D) Co. Ltd. on 31st December, 1976

	£	£		£
Issued preference shares		20,000	Fixed assets	79,000
Issued ordinary shares of £1		50,000	Current assets	7,000
Revenue reserve at 1/1/76		8,000		
Profit and loss account:				
at 30/9/76	1,500			
1/10/76 to 31/12/76	500			
		2,000		
Loan from 'H'		3,000		
Current liabilities		3,000		
		86,000		86,000

Calculation of goodwill by an alternative approach to exhibit 3–2 is as follows:

	£	£
Purchase price		40,000
less: Net assets purchased:		
Nominal value of acquired shares	30,000	
Revenue reserve purchased 60% × £8,000	4,800	
Profit purchased 60% × £1,500	900	
		35,700
Goodwill		4,300

Minority interest is therefore:

	£	£
Preference shares		20,000
Ordinary shares 20,000 @ £1	20,000	
Revenue reserve 40% × £8,000	3,200	
Profit: 40% × £1,500	600	
AND 40% × £500	200	
		24,000
Minority Interest		44,000

Consolidated Balance Sheet of 'H' Co. Ltd. and S(D) Co. Ltd.
on 31st December, 1976

	£		£
Issued ordinary shares	100,000	Fixed assets	134,000
Profit and loss account		Goodwill	4,300
S(D) from 1/10/76 – 60% of £500	300[1]	Current assets	19,000
Minority interest	44,000		
Current liabilities	13,000		
	157,300		157,300

When studying published consolidated balance sheets, two items commonly found which refer to the purchase of subsidiary companies, namely minority interests and goodwill on consolidation, should now be clear. What has happened, then, is that all assets and current liabilities of subsidiaries have been added to the holding company's balances, the value of these items belonging to share-holders who have not sold their shares to the holding company, is deducted as a liability to minority interests, and any excess the company has paid for net assets taken over has been added as goodwill.

The shares bought by the holding company will have been paid for in shares, debentures or cash or some combination of these.

The balance sheet of the holding company only shows interests in subsidiary companies as an asset, and therefore presents few problems in preparation.

Consolidated Profit and Loss Accounts

The preparation of these naturally follows a similar pattern to that required for consolidating the balance sheet, in that the group's figures are added together and necessary adjustments made to them. To be more specific:

 (a) Previous years' undistributed profit of all companies making up the group *is added to*

 (b) The past years' profit of all the group.

   from which is subtracted (c), (d), (e) and (f) below:

 (c) Pre-acquisition profits of the subsidiary.

 (d) Profits of the subsidiary belonging to minority interests.

 (e) Unrealized profit on inter-company transfers.

 (f) Inter-company dividends.

Exhibit 3–5

Showing the preparation of a consolidated profit and loss account covering the above points.

H(A) Co. Ltd. bought on 1st January, 1976, 12,000 ordinary shares in S(E) Co. Ltd. out of a total of 16,000. Stock of S(E) includes £1,000 for goods

---

[1] This represents 'H's' share of profit made by S(D) since acquisition.

invoiced by H(A) at cost + 25%. The following profit and loss accounts were extracted before eliminating the inter-company profit in the stock held.

Profit and Loss Accounts for year ended 31st December, 1976

	H(A) £	S(E) £		H(A) £	S(E) £
Interim dividends paid	10,000	4,000	Balance b/f	20,000	6,000
Balance c/f	29,000	10,000	Net profit for year	16,000	8,000
			Interim dividend from S(E)	3,000	
	39,000	14,000		39,000	14,000

Notes on accounts above and below:
1. H(A) Co. Ltd. has a 75% interest in S(E) Co. Ltd. leaving a 25% minority interest.
2. Profit included in stock valuation is £200.
   (Cost of £800 + 25% profit = £1,000). Since the stock is partly owned by minority shareholders, that portion is regarded as being sold to outsiders and the related profit counted as part of group profit. Profit to be eliminated is therefore 75% of £200.

Much of the detailed consolidation work is not shown in published group profit and loss accounts, reference being limited usually to minority interests.

Consolidated Profit and Loss Account of H(A) Co. Ltd. with S(E) Co. Ltd. for year ended 31st December, 1976

	£	£		£	£
Dividend paid by S(E)	4,000		Balance b/f		
Less minority interest	1,000		S(E)	6,000 (a)	
			Less minority interest	1,500 (c)	
	3,000 (f)			4,500	
Less contra	3,000		H(A)	20,000 (a)	
		—			24,500
Dividend paid by H(A)		10,000	Net profit for year S(E)	8,000 (b)	
Profit on goods sold to S(E)	200		Less minority Interest	2,000 (d)	
Less minority interest	50 (e)			6,000	
		150	H(A)	16,000 (b)	
Balance c/f					22,000
S(E)	10,000		Interim dividend from S(E)	3,000 (f)	
Less minority Interest	2,500 (c)&(d)		Less contra	3,000	
	7,500				—
Less stock adjustment	150 (e)				
	7,350				
H(A)	29,000				
		36,350			
		46,500			46,500

A.F.M./2—D

Associated Company

A company holding 50% or less ordinary share capital in another company may be said to have an investment in an associated company.

Questions and Problems

3–1 Show the consolidated balance sheet as at 30th April, 1976.

PARENT COMPANY

Balance Sheet as at 30th April, 1976

	£		£
Capital	6,000	Investment in S. Ltd. at cost	
Profit loss A/c	3,500	1,000 shares	1,600
Creditors	1,500	Fixed assets	5,400
		Current assets	4,000
	11,000		11,000

SUBSIDIARY COMPANY

Balance Sheet as at 30th April, 1976

	£		£
Capital	1,000	Fixed assets	1,800
Profit and loss A/c	350	Current assets	750
Creditors	1,200		
	2,550		2,550

3–2 The following are the balance sheets of A. Ltd. and its subsidiary B. Ltd. On the date when A. Ltd. acquired the shares in B. Ltd., the latter company had a credit balance on the profit and loss account of £5,000. Prepare the consolidated balance sheet at 31st March, 1977.

A. LTD.

Balance Sheet at 31st March, 1977

	£		£
Capital – 270,000 £1 shares	270,000	Freehold land and buildings at cost	100,000
Creditors	10,000	Investment in B. Ltd. at cost (144,000 shares)	144,000
		Stock	25,000
		Debtors	3,000
		Balance at bank	8,000
	280,000		280,000

B. LTD.
Balance Sheet as at 31st March, 1977

	£		£
Capital – 200,000 £1 shares	200,000	Freehold land and	
Profit and loss A/c	1,500	buildings at cost	150,000
Creditors	43,500	Stock	50,000
		Debtors	30,000
		Balance at bank	15,000
	245,000		245,000

3–3 The balance sheet of A. Ltd. on 31st December was:

	£		£
Share capital	14,000	Fixed assets	10,000
Debentures	2,500	Investment in B. Ltd.	
Profit and loss A/c	2,000	4,000 shares at cost	5,200
Creditors	1,500	Current assets	4,800
	20,000		20,000

The balance sheet of B. Ltd. on 31st December was:

	£		£
Ordinary shares capital	5,000	Fixed assets	5,000
6% preference shares	2,500	Current assets	4,200
Profit and loss A/c	1,000		
Creditors	700		
	9,200		9,200

On the date when A. Ltd. acquired the shares in B. Ltd., the profit and loss account of B. Ltd. stood at £500 (Cr). No dividends have been paid during the year but one year's dividend due to the preference shareholders has not yet been provided for. Prepare the consolidated balance sheet.

3–4 The accounts of A. Ltd. and its subsidiary B. Ltd. are shown below. A. Ltd. acquired its holding in B. Ltd. two years ago when the balance on B. Ltd.'s profit and loss account was £800. Prepare consolidated profit and loss account and balance sheet. (Ignore taxation.)

Profit and Loss Accounts
For the year ended 31st December, 1976

	A. Ltd. £	B. Ltd. £		A. Ltd. £	B. Ltd. £
Auditors' remuneration	200	100	Trading profit	3,000	1,600
Depreciation	300	200	Dividend – B. Ltd.	300	
Directors' fees	1,000	400			
Net profit c/d.	1,800	900			
	3,300	1,600		3,300	1,600
Income tax	800	380	Balance b/fwd.	550	1,700
Proposed div'd (Gross)	550	220	Net profit b/d.	1,800	900
Balance c/d.	1,000	2,000			
	2,350	2,600		2,350	2,600

Balance Sheet as at 31st December, 1976

	A. Ltd.	B. Ltd.		A. Ltd.	B. Ltd.
Authorized & issued capital	9,000	3,000	Fixed assets	5,000	3,000
Profit & loss account	1,000	2,000	3,000 shares in B. Ltd. at		
B. Ltd.	500		cost	4,000	
Sundry creditors	950	780	Current assets	3,000	2,500
Proposed dividend	550	220	A. Ltd.		500
	12,000	6,000		12,000	6,000

Note: The Stocks of B. Ltd. include £600 goods supplied by A. Ltd., the cost to the latter company being £500.

CHAPTER FOUR

INTRODUCTION TO FINANCIAL PLANNING AND CONTROL

PROFIT is achieved by the effective management of all available resources, which are basically people and finance, and an important aim of the accounting function is to supply information that will aid management in the effective use of such resources. A management accounting system, accordingly, provides information on which managers can better manage, and because it measures profit and decisions affecting profit, should embrace all matters stated in monetary terms.

Planning Aspects

Much management accounting work involves the preparation of routine statements to show whether the business is running as planned, an important function, but one which is rendered relatively ineffective if the plan itself is poor. A frequent business failing is the inability to be adaptive at management level although first-class routine control information is provided at the operating level. The result is effective performance of bad plans.

This situation may be illustrated by comparing the results of Restaurants A and B for a 12-month period (year 2) shown in Exhibit 4–1.

Exhibit 4–1

PROFIT STATEMENT

	Year 1 Actual		Year 2 Budget		Year 2 Actual	
Restaurant A	£	%	£	%	£	%
Revenue	17,000	100	20,000	100	19,000	100
Food costs	8,500	50	10,000	50	9,800	52
GROSS MARGIN	8,500	50	10,000	50	9,200	48
Other costs	5,000	29	5,000	25	5,000	26
PROFIT	3,500	21	5,000	25	4,200	22
Restaurant B						
Revenue	17,000	100	17,000	100	17,400	100
Food costs	8,500	50	8,500	50	8,700	50
GROSS MARGIN	8,500	50	8,500	50	8,700	50
Other costs	5,000	29	5,000	29	5,000	29
PROFIT		3,50021	3,500	21	3,700	21

Restaurant 'A's' management planned to improve profit from £3,500 in year 1 to £5,000 in year 2, but in the event, turnover fell short of budget and food costs increased to 52% of sales, resulting in a profit of £4,200.

Restaurant 'B's' management pursued a policy of no change, concentrating its efforts on repeating year 1 results. Although food costs were controlled to 50% of sales, turnover increased and profit was £200 above year 1.

Which restaurant would you say was better managed?

To give a sensible answer requires a study of facts not present in this simple profit statement, although it might be said that if all other financial factors, such as working capital and property values, were identical, then Restaurant 'A's' management did the better job in increasing profit by £700 in the year compared with 'B's' increase of only £200.

Factors to be taken into account in assessing the results of A and B would include:

1. If A's profit has been achieved without additional investment, e.g. by better service or a pricing policy change, then existing resources have been more effectively managed and A's management is probably better than B's.
2. If A spent £20,000 on additional facilities in the year, the extra return of £700 ($3\frac{1}{2}$%) might be regarded as a disappointment. However, the payoff may be expected in year 3 and A's management may therefore be reasonably satisfied with year 2 results.
3. How are future profits likely to be affected by decisions taken in the year? A decision not to redecorate might adversely affect year 3 turnover and therefore profit.
4. Is the business in a position to settle its suppliers' bills as they fall due? A might not, even though an improved profit has been recorded. Sight of the balance sheet might help with this answer.
5. From what sources have finances been obtained? One restaurant may be paying more for its capital than the other because of poor management.
6. Has the increase in food costs of A been the result of a policy change, increased food prices, or increased wastage? If wastage is the cause then management has been at fault.
7. What has been the rate of inflation in the year? If 6% occurred in year 2 B might be worse off than in year 1 because £210 extra profit would be required to offset the fall in the value of money.

Most of these questions and many more can be answered by means of a good management accounting system which helps to quantify the effect of management plans and results.

It might be argued that management of restaurant B has failed to be adaptive in not benefiting sufficiently from an expanding market, partly through too much attention to the control side. In the 1960s, Trust Houses suffered on the one hand because there was no forward plan for the group as a whole, and on the other hand, the detailed control over hotel managers was so tight that it destroyed initiative.

It is clear in modern management where competition is keen, that the successful management is flexible in outlook, plans with care yet takes calculated risks, trying to anticipate its customers' requirements, the labour market and availability of finance.

How then can an understanding of the financial side of the business help the manager to plan more effectively? Basically in two ways:

(a) Participating in routine annual budgeting will highlight important relationships existing between management functions, co-ordination of which help in smooth running of operations and optimization of profit.

(b) Participating in the preparation of statements showing the effect on overall business profit of alternative courses of action, will give the manager confidence in seeking profitable opportunities.

The extent to which (a) and (b) above are formalized depends upon the size of the business, for the smaller undertaking will require a simple system; yet these two parts of the planning operation, routine budgeting and ad hoc profit studies, are relevant to even the smallest business.

It will be seen that at any time a business opportunity may be discovered which, when evaluated in terms of return on investment, is either rejected or accepted as falling in line with laid down policy and built into the next budget.

Planning for profit involves not only seeing that there is a surplus of revenue over costs, but also that sufficient cash and stock is available when needed, and that finance is obtained from the right source, i.e. that expansion involving purchase of accommodation and other long-term assets is not paid for by short-term credit, but from long-term sources such as the issue of shares, debentures and retained profit. The oldest financial mistake in the world is borrowing short-term and investing long-term.

Control Considerations

Whilst the importance of a good plan is stressed, *control* of costs, revenue, stocks, and cash is essential in order to avoid unnecessary loss and wastage leading to falling profit. Hotel and catering businesses are generally alive to the needs of good control routines, especially when concerned with the day to day control of food, sales and cash where underages and overages can be quickly identified and speedy action taken to bring the position back into control if at all possible. Such control procedures are largely to avoid fraudulent use of the assets involved, but are only a part, although an important part, of the overall control system of the business which aims to help supervisors and managers achieve planned results. Results need to be quantified for comparison with planned performance and may be, for example, number of portions for day to day control. Somewhere along the line the measurement must be in value as it flows through the management accounting system so that management can see the overall picture of departmental and company performance.

This overall picture is achieved by means of an operating statement which shows actual and budgeted departmental revenues and costs and other hotel income and costs; in other words it is a profit and loss statement used for control purposes. An attempt is made to use budgets to help those responsible to control revenue and costs at departmental and hotel levels. Exhibit 4–2 shows a pro forma operating statement with control levels recommended in N.E.D.O.s *A Standard System of Hotel Accounting.* Since any change in revenue or cost directly affects planned profit, investigation of the significant variances is most important to enable management to rectify the position if results are adverse or to exploit the position if results become favourable. A significant adverse food cost caused by a national price rise might call for selling price revision whereas a favourable turnover compared with budget, after investigation may lead to the discovery of an untapped source of customers.

Control of assets such as cash and stocks is aided only to a limited extent by comparison between actual and budget figures, since this only indicates whether policy in relation to levels of cash and stock holding is being achieved. More important, as mentioned earlier, is the stewardship function in maintaining accurate records of purchases and sales and ensuring that adequate physical control is exercised to avoid fraud.

Monthly and cumulative operating statements showing value and percentages

Exhibit 4–2

FORM OF OPERATING STATEMENT WITH CONTROL LEVELS

Item	Person initially responsible	Control period	Method of control
Departmental net sales *Less:* cost of sales	Room, Food & Beverage Managers	Daily	Cash and credit sales records. Weekly/monthly summary Food & beverage control
Departmental gross profit *Less:* wages and staff costs	Room, Food & Beverage Managers	Monthly	Operated departmental comparison of budget with actual expenses
Departmental net margin *Less:* direct departmental expenses	Room, Food & Beverage Managers	Monthly	Operated departmental comparison of budget with actual expenses
Departmental operating profit *Less:* service & general apportioned expenses	Service Department Managers	Monthly	Comparison of service departmental budgets with actual expenses
Hotel gross operating profit *Less:* provision of plant and accommodation **Hotel net operating profit**	Hotel Manager Hotel Manager	Quarterly Annually	Expenditure fixed in nature and controlled largely by policy decision

help to indicate how the business is performing against budget, and may be said to be an internal control mechanism.

In recent years control has been aided by comparison with other hotels of percentages and ratios designed to indicate one's position relative to other similar establishments. This external control facility illustrates the continuing communication between the planning and control functions, for the greatest benefit is the guide management receives in setting better targets in areas where the business is producing a relatively poor performance.

Questions and Problems

4–1   Explain why a good financial plan is important to any business regardless of size of the undertaking.

4–2   A profit plan needs to ensure not only that sufficient profit will result, but also that there will be enough stock and cash available. Is a lack of cash more critical than making a loss? Explain.

4–3   Using assumed figures, explain why a business which has fallen short of a planned profit may be in a more satisfactory position than another business which has successfully repeated last year's results.

4–4   Should the current year's profit be the sole criterion of a successful management? Explain.

4–5   In a large hotel, which managers can influence the level of the following costs – food, kitchen wages, local rates of the kitchen, replacement of glass and china, maintenance of kitchen equipment?

CHAPTER FIVE

COST CHARACTERISTICS

THE object of this chapter is to explain basic cost characteristics and to give some idea of the uses of cost information. All levels of management are concerned with costs either in a dynamic situation making decisions, or in a more mundane manner keeping costs under control. In any event an understanding of costs, and especially their behaviour in relation to quantity of output, goes a long way towards using costs correctly to further the aims of the enterprise. The word 'cost' can rarely stand alone and should be qualified to ensure its meaning is faithfully communicated. It is the amount of expenditure incurred for some specific purpose.

Classification of Costs

There are several ways of classifying cost, depending upon the object of the exercise. For the present purpose only three need be demonstrated as shown in Exhibit 5–1.

Basic Elements of Cost

This is the simplest form of classification and is a convenient means of assembling costs to offset revenue in a Profit and Loss account.

Direct and Indirect Costs

Here begins a classification used for management purposes. The cost of direct materials, e.g. food, taken away from food sales gives the all important gross profit percentage. Direct wages taken away from gross profit shows departmental net margin. These residual figures are important checks on departmental profitability. Expenses are mainly indirect which together with indirect material and indirect labour are sometimes called overhead or burden (U.S.A. term). Direct costs are those which can be directly related to a product, saleable service or department.

Fixed and Variable Costs

This classification is immensely important and much attention will be paid to it elsewhere. Initially definitions will provide a basic knowledge of this classification.

Form	Basic cost elements	Direct and indirect	Fixed and variable
Purpose	Basic records for simple profit statement	Relating costs to departments for cost and profit control	Showing response to activity changes for various planning and control purposes

Total cost

Materials used

Wages

Expenses

DIRECT
Materials used
— — — — —
Direct wages
— — — — —
Direct expenses

INDIRECT
Materials
— — — — —
Wages
— — — — —
Expenses

Variable costs

Semi–variable costs

Fixed costs

Variable cost: a cost which in total tends to vary in direct proportion to changes in volume of activity in a period. Activity refers to some productive activity such as dishes prepared, meals served, rooms occupied. An undisputed variable cost is the cost of food.

Fixed cost: a cost which accrues in relation to the passage of time and which tends to be unaffected by fluctuations in volume of activity in a period. Such costs as local rates, rent, manager's basic salary are clearly fixed costs.

Semi-variable cost: a cost containing both fixed and variable elements which is therefore partly affected by fluctuations in volume of activity in a period. A large number of costs fall into this category such as wages, electricity and laundry.

This classification does not usually feature in the routine accounting system largely because of the highly subjective nature of the split between fixed and variable categories. The few firms in other industries who do have this classification in their system would refer to it as a Marginal Costing System.

Cost Behaviour – Volume
For the purpose of illustrating various cost behaviour patterns relating to volume it is usual to measure the monetary value of cost on the vertical (y) axis and volume along the horizontal or (x) axis. Timescale is not usually depicted but a 12-month period is often assumed. Some examples of costs on cost/volume charts are shown below.

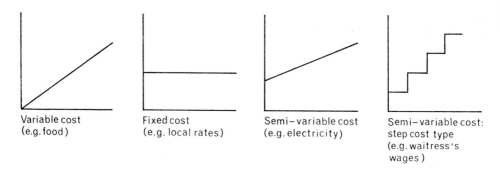

Variable cost (e.g. food)   Fixed cost (e.g. local rates)   Semi–variable cost (e.g. electricity)   Semi–variable cost: step cost type (e.g. waitress's wages)

Many types of semi-variable cost patterns result from changes in volume of activity. One such is the step cost where another waitress has to be engaged who will serve a small range of extra covers, all for her extra wage – the rise in the 'step'. For practical purposes, the width of the 'step' will determine whether the cost may be regarded as variable or fixed. For example, in the case of the waitresses' wages the underlying behaviour pattern would be regarded as variable. These patterns show cost changes resulting from changes in volume of activity so that inflation, for instance, has to be considered separately.

Cost Behaviour – Semi-Variable Cost
The benefits from having the first two categories, fixed and variable, are numerous and are considered in Chapter 8, but the problem arises of placing all costs into these two categories. The semi-variable category has to be eliminated and there are several methods of apportioning these costs to the fixed and variable categories. In each case care is needed to ensure that costs taken from different points in time have had inflation effects removed.

(a) Technical assessment
Often the person closely involved with the cost item can give a fair estimate of the cost behaviour such as the chef estimating the variability in usage of some indirect foods.

(b) High and low points method
By taking the highest and lowest costs of a series of periods, it is assumed that the difference represents the variable costs related to the change in volume of activity. A cost related to meals prepared has records to show that over 12 periods the highest and lowest period costs were £642 and £603 with corresponding number of meals being 3,157 and 2,878 respectively. The variable cost calculation is as follows:

		Total costs £	No. meals
Highest cost – period 10		642	3,157
Lowest cost – period 2		603	2,878
	Difference	£39	279
Variable cost per unit	=	£39	÷ 279 = £0·14
Fixed cost can be calculated:		£	
Total cost period 10		642	
Variable cost = 3,157 × £0·14 =		442	
Fixed cost =		200	

Clearly a cost/volume chart could be drawn, using a suitable scale, to depict this by inserting one point for each period and joining the two points, extending them also to the (y) axis. The chart would appear:

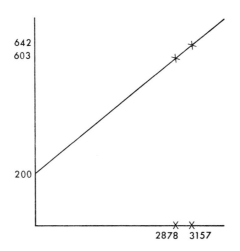

(c) Scattergraph or chart
This tends to be more accurate than the high and low method in that here all the 12 points available from a series of recordings are plotted instead of just

two. A straight line (line of best fit) is drawn through the points in such a manner that it passes roughly midway between them. Again, on meeting the (y) axis, the fixed cost component is determined.

(*d*) Method of least squares:
This is a statistical calculation that results in a technically accurate line of best fit or a regression line.

It will be noted, the three methods using past records assume that a straight line represents the cost changes, and this may not necessarily be true.

Fixed costs are fairly easy to identify, and apart from food, liquor and other direct sales, there are few truly variable costs, which simplifies their determination. The separation of semi-variable into fixed and variable categories is admittedly a rather imperfect exercise. It is nevertheless true that the accuracy obtained has been sufficient for many successful cost analyses used in decision making.

Cost Behaviour – Other Influences
(*a*) Variable costs: Among the more important factors, which influence total cost in a period of an item like food are:
1. Volume and mix of dishes served
2. Price paid for food including seasonal variations and inflation
3. Quality of food
4. Quantity lost between delivering and serving
5. Quantity of food in each dish
It can be seen that in the rather extreme case of food cost, a large number of assumptions are made when a straight line is shown to represent the way a variable cost rises in response to volume changes. On the other hand standards may and generally are set for each factor to assist the control of food costs and these can be assumed to hold good during a period, leaving volume the one factor to account for in planning.
(*b*) Fixed costs: Charts depicting fixed costs are usually for 12 months, the common planning period. If two consecutive years were to be depicted, then a step cost would be shown, the result of expected inflation in the second year. Expansion in the second year would also be a cause of a rise in fixed costs. In the longer term therefore, what is recognized as a fixed cost would become semi-variable. Some fixed costs which are the result of policy decisions can be varied almost at will, namely training costs, advertising and research. However, they would still be regarded as fixed in relation to a 12-month policy.

Correct Use of Cost Information
In using cost information there is the danger of using the wrong cost in a management decision and of not seeing the wood for the trees. Generally, the simple approach is best by taking account of the relevant information and ignoring all irrelevant information. For instance, the use of incremental or differential costs and revenue – those which would change if a decision were

taken – avoids having to bother about many other costs and revenue which would not change. The following shows how costs may be used in decision making.

Irrelevance of Historical Costs

Decisions cannot alter the past and are entirely concerned with the future. The monetary information relevant to a decision are expected future costs and revenues, and where appropriate, future capital spending. Historical costs and book values of fixed assets are not relevant. Past figures may be used as a guide to future costs and revenues, but as a guide only. Past costs should not be used in a calculation to help in a decision.

Irrelevance of Some Future Costs

This sounds strange, but in the right context can avoid clouding an issue. A decision involving a comparison of alternative future costs may be hindered by the inclusion of those costs, mainly fixed costs, which in total are not going to be affected by the decision. There is the classic case of the hotel group closing an hotel because it was reckoned to be unprofitable. However, included in its costs was a charge for central administration services which pushed the hotel into the red. The result was that after the closure the group profit fell instead of rising because the central services expenses remained unchanged, and the group lost the surplus of the hotel's income over its own costs. The future expenses of the central services were irrelevant to the decision because in total they were not expected to change.

Decisions Should Improve Group Profit

Although this sounds trite it is easy to overlook. A decision which increases hotel profit may be made at the expense of group profit and similarly an increased department gross profit may reduce hotel profit. It is particularly appropriate to take care when there is inter-company trading requiring internal transfer prices to be set.

Selling Below Cost

A common fallacy is never to sell below cost. It will be seen that long-term prices must be set above cost, but short term, not to be repeated, prices like summer sales in fashion houses may be below cost. Original cost is irrelevant here where stock needs to be moved. Opportunity cost, or the market price becomes the operative cost.

Interest as a Cost

Decisions which involve significant capital spending and change the pattern of future cost and revenues beyond say two years demand that interest on capital be taken into account. A technique known as Discounted Cash Flow (DCF) is now accepted by many as the most appropriate way of dealing with interest in making investment decisions.

Unquantifiable Costs and Benefits
It should always be borne in mind that not all factors bearing on a decision can be quantified. Other factors may be judged to override calculated financial advantages. For example, although it may be shown that hotels receiving convenience food from a subsidiary rather than outside the group involves the group in a loss, this may be acceptable on the grounds that it widens the market for the food and is a form of advertising. The benefits are not quantifiable. Other factors may be convenience, certainty of supplies, helping to keep together a work force.

Value of Accounting Information
The value of information to an organization should exceed the cost of obtaining it. This is undoubtedly a rule which is very difficult to support with figures, because of the subjective nature of 'value' and the difficulty of costing information. Yet consciously or otherwise those in business tend to use this rule, and it is particularly true in management accounting which is essentially concerned with obtaining and presenting economic information to management. The effect of this rule is to constrain the urge in some quarters to amass more and more data, for it does not become information until it is communicated and often too much data means less really gets through as information.

An hotel group which expanded rapidly would be unwise not to introduce a standard system of accounting in which budgets were uniformly prepared and compared with actual results. The value of the improved financial control resulting would be likely to outweigh the cost of operating the system. Lack of financial control information has been the downfall of a number of expanding companies. An instance, however, where the cost exceeds the value is in the area of cost behaviour. An hotel group might spend £100,000 annually in order to set up and operate a system which predicted more accurately than before how each cost would change during the coming year. Its value would be very real in having a more accurate profit plan and cost control data, but the value would be incapable of accurate numerical assessment. This kind of system does not operate in the industry today because it would be regarded as uneconomic. Just to recover the extra annual cost, cost savings of £100,000 per annum would be needed from elsewhere in the group or extra turnover of say £300,000 per annum would be needed as a direct result of the better information provided.

Inevitably cost information in terms of behaviour is a compromise, and judgement is needed to assess the level of accuracy acceptable.

Budgetary Control
(a) Planning
It will be seen later than an enterprise needs to plan its operations, revenues and costs for a 12-month period at least, to enable a realistic profit target to be set and acted upon. Knowing the cost behaviour pattern of each cost enables a forecast of costs for each department and for the company to be prepared at different levels of activity. These can then be adjusted to forecast inflation. A

monthly operating plan is in this way prepared to cover a 12-month period. A detailed study of this is in Chapter 6.

(b) Control

The benefits of a plan do not end with planning. At the end of each month an overall check is required to determine whether costs have matched expectations and by adjusting the planned costs to take account of the actual activity achieved in the month a useful comparison can be made with actual results. Further, by recognizing that food is a variable cost, very close control can be exercised in the kitchen of food-biased establishments by using Standard Costing, a technique which operates as an extension of Budgetary Control.

Costs in Perspective

It must be said that when compared with some industries like light engineering and oil refining, the hotel and catering industry appears to have less complex

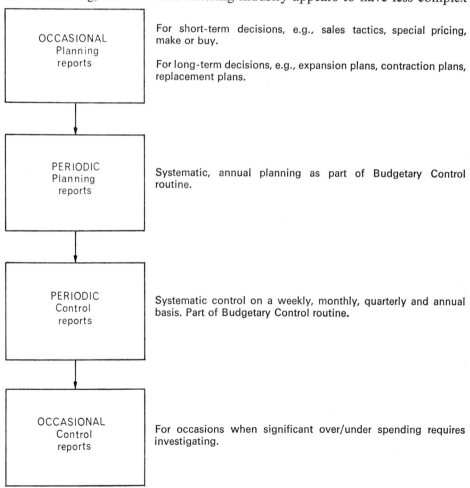

OCCASIONAL Planning reports — For short-term decisions, e.g., sales tactics, special pricing, make or buy.

For long-term decisions, e.g., expansion plans, contraction plans, replacement plans.

PERIODIC Planning reports — Systematic, annual planning as part of Budgetary Control routine.

PERIODIC Control reports — Systematic control on a weekly, monthly, quarterly and annual basis. Part of Budgetary Control routine.

OCCASIONAL Control reports — For occasions when significant over/under spending requires investigating.

cost problems than other industries. Hotel and catering units are generally smaller, do not hold finished stocks and operations are fewer. This is fortunate in that management should be in a good position to understand cost problems and to take advantage of techniques herein described if they appear relevant.

Cost behaviour – the response of cost to a variety of influences – is said to be the most important single aspect of sound cost planning and control.

Cost planning and sales planning go hand in hand for they combine to form a company's profit target.

Management Accounting Reports

There are basically two kinds of management accounting report which reflect the different work involved.

Periodic Reports

These are systematically compiled and presented at regular intervals as part of the Budgetary Control System.

Occasional Reports

These are prepared when the occasion demands and usually relate to either 'What would happen to profit if we did this?' kind of question, or reasons for results not conforming to plan, e.g. how has inflation affected budgeted profit?

Questions and Problems

5–1 Explain what you understand by the 'elements of cost'.

5–2 Distinguish between 'direct' and 'indirect' costs and give examples of each.

5–3 Distinguish between 'fixed' and 'variable' costs.

5–4 Why is it necessary to distinguish fixed costs from variable costs?

5–5 What is a semi-variable cost?

5–6 Outline the various methods of identifying the fixed and variable elements of semi-variable costs.

5–7 'In the long term all costs are variable'. Explain.

5–8 A prospective client visited a banqueting suite to acquire a suitable menu quotation for his firm's annual dinner. For a single menu he was given the following quotations:

		selling price per head £
Menu 'D'	100 covers	3·00
Menu 'D'	150 covers	2·80
Menu 'D'	200 covers	2·65

Portion size and quality of the food and service being the same in all cases. Explain how it is possible for a banqueting suite to reduce the selling price per head simply because of an increase in the number of covers, and yet maintain the same net profit-to-sales ratio.

5–9 Sketch a graph from which could be read the *cost per unit* at various levels of activity in respect of:
    (*a*) variable cost
    (*b*) fixed cost
    (*c*) total cost
Draw the three cost lines and label each one.

5–10 Below are details of a number of costs:
    1. Spirits used up at a constant cost per measure.
    2. Electricity charge consisting of a flat basic charge plus a variable charge after a minimum number of units have been used.
    3. Depreciation of equipment where the charge is calculated by the straight line method.
    4. Salaries of maintenance staff where 1 member of staff is required for 150 bedrooms or less, 2 members of staff for 151–300 bedrooms, 3 members of staff for 301–450 bedrooms and so on.
    5. Cost of wine in bulk, where the cost per litre decreases with each litre until a minimum cost per litre is reached.
    6. Laundry costs in an hotel which changes all its bedroom linen after each bednight.

You are to match each cost with its relevant graph.

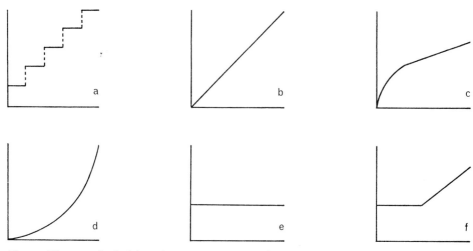

Note: The vertical (y) axis represents total cost and the horizontal (x) axis represents total activity.

5–11 Below are details of a number of costs:
1. Local rates.
2. Gas charge which consists of a standing charge for the service itself plus a variable charge per unit, for all units used.
3. Food used up in the preparation of meals at a constant cost per kilo.
4. Wages of banqueting waiters where 1 waiter is required for every 10 covers or less, 2 waiters for 11–20 covers, 3 waiters for 21–30 covers etc.
5. Rental of taped music equipment.
Sketch five graphs (not necessarily to scale) to match each of the five costs.

Further Reading
1. Baggott, J., *Cost and Management Accounting*, W. H. Allen; chapter 3.
2. Horngren, C. T., *Cost Accounting: A managerial emphasis*, Prentice-Hall; chapter 8.
3. Sizer, J., *An Insight Into Management Accounting*, Penguin Books; chapter 10.

CHAPTER SIX

BUDGETARY PLANNING

Budgetary Control

One accepted definition of budgetary control is:

(*a*) the establishment of budgets relating the responsibility of executives to the requirement of a policy, and

(*b*) the continuous comparison of actual and budgeted results,

(*c*) either to secure by individual action the objective of that policy,

(*d*) or to provide a basis for its (the budget) revision.

Any definition contains the same essential ingredients,

The following chart (Exhibit 6–1) illustrates this definition and shows that

Exhibit 6–1

OUTLINE BUDGETARY CONTROL CHART

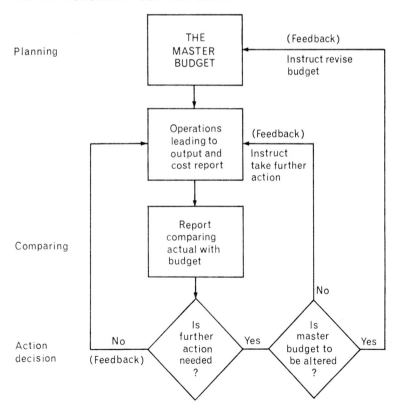

feedback is designed to trigger off action by advising the planners to change the budget or the operating personnel to take remedial action.

The approach made in considering budgetary control is to explain the planning side in this chapter and control aspects in the following chapter.

Planning Levels

Three planning levels are operated in the successful business, viz:

Strategic planning which is concerned with the objectives of the enterprise and the long-range plans required to achieve such objectives. Top management takes strategic planning decisions.

Management control which concerns middle management obtaining and employing resources effectively within the framework of strategic planning decisions.

Operational planning and control which is concerned with planning day-to-day work capable of fairly close control.

These levels concern general management and are introduced here to put budgetary control in perspective. The following is an attempt to equate these levels with Financial Management and Management Accounting work and it will be seen that only the lowest level is outside our terms of reference.

		Accounting involvement
Strategic planning	—	Long-term budgeting (over 12 months)
Management control	—	Budgetary control – the 12-month cycle
Operational control	—	Limited involvement

The above functions exist in any business and in the small business the owner may carry out all of these functions with few paperwork aids, but the larger the enterprise the more specialists are required to carry out these functions.

It has been said that one factor that differentiates the top manager from the operative is the length of time which transpires before decisions made by them are proved to be the right ones. The top manager who decides to build a new hotel in order to extend business does not know the outcome for several years when profits and cash flows are compared with his own estimates. The waiter's decision to serve one person before another may be a wrong one, and there is an immediate response. His decision has but little effect on business profit. The top manager's decision may lose or gain the business thousands of pounds.

Long-Term Budgets

The business which returns to the owner a continuing adequate profit will most likely have a management which has not been content with making just day-to-day plans, but has looked further ahead and anticipated changes in customer demands and made preparations to meet them. Airline businesses would go to the wall if they failed to anticipate the number of passengers expected to use particular routes in 12 months' time, bearing in mind current trends and known changes likely to affect the future position, e.g. extensive hotel development where passengers disembark. Besides, new aircraft have to be ordered years in advance of delivery making it essential that plans are laid in good time.

We see here the basis of two important forecasts, that of sales and of aircraft (capital equipment), required in the airline industry. Yet a business with relatively static sales, such as a biscuit manufacturer needs to forecast sales and indeed to influence sales, so that the most profitable sales mix is achieved. New lines may have to be introduced requiring experiment and the purchase of capital equipment. Unless profitable opportunities are taken by a business, competitors will take advantage of them.

The significance of the long-term planning function depends upon the industry and size of business within the industry. The huge airline corporations rely on expensively produced long- and short-term plans, whereas the smaller charter aircraft business may flourish with less sophisticated planning. So with the hotel and catering industry, the large hotel group requires relatively more and elaborate planning than the small restaurant.

Several forecasts, each covering sales, capital expenditure, finance and profit would be provided by the planners for a period of say five years, but based on different assumptions as to sales levels and gross margins, possible hotel sites, and methods of financing the expansion. The board of directors will satisfy themselves that one of the forecasts is likely to best carry forward their strategic plan and they would make this forecast the basis of their policy for the next five years. The forecast has become a budget because it is now the company's policy to carry out the plans contained in the forecast. This long-term budget will inevitably be only approximate and will be altered from year to year, but it is a target that the top management will constantly have in their sights, confident that when it was made it was the best available, and certainly a feasible one.

The foregoing applies to the larger enterprise, although the management of the smaller business will still consider possible changes in the next few years, but their sales, profit and capital expenditure projections may not be formalized as budgets, only recorded as memoranda to be considered when appropriate.

The first year of the five-year budget will be used to guide the planners in preparing the short-term 12-month budget which is the start of detailed budgetary control procedures.

Limiting Factors

The top manager's decision is part of a long-term plan which usually involves changes in the company's interest in fixed assets whereby a forecast demand for rooms in a district is satisfied by the building and operation of an hotel. Here we see a forecast of sales and a forecast of capital expenditure, which would demand a forecast of finance to ensure cash was available.

The planning function of the hotel group will consider factors likely to affect the industry generally in the coming few years, such as accelerated economic growth of the country; upward movement in family income groups leading to more discretionary spending power; increase in number of married women workers; increased mobility of population and increase in numbers of tourists.

The planners would then consider how these factors would affect the hotel group's turnover and profit. They would quickly discover one or more limiting factors, this is to say factors the extent of whose influence must be first assessed in order to ensure that other parts of the plan are reasonably capable of fulfilment. A sudden boom in trade would result in accommodation being the limiting factor, a situation which arose in London in 1969 when several million more visitors arrived than were expected. This limiting factor was partially overcome following requests by the B.T.A. for people outside the industry to put up those failing to find accommodation in hotels. Relating this to the business it can be seen that it is an important function of management to anticipate a limiting factor and to eliminate it, although inevitably another one takes its place.

In the long term, sales will be the limiting factor so that sales will be the first forecast, followed by the capital expenditure which will provide the facilities required to achieve the forecast sales. At the same time finance will be forecast to provide for the purchase or lease of the facilities. Besides sales other limiting factors may be space for accommodation or seating, labour of the right kind, finance for expansion, or even management itself may be a limiting factor in that it has not the capacity to meet the demands of the business.

Short-Term Budgets
The immediate few months ahead are of vital interest to all management and detailed plans would be prepared covering such matters as staff recruitment, equipment replacement, maintenance, advertising, food and accommodation pricing, stock levels, banking arrangements to name some of the items to be considered. One proven method of seeing that these arrangements are co-ordinated and comprehensive is to express them in monetary form; in other words a budget is produced. This we have seen is a plan to assist in the direction of resources and trading activities of a business in order to achieve a given objective and can be used to assist in the control of resources and activities.

A convenient period for a budget is 12 months since this covers a full cycle of activities; is a short enough period to plan in detail; and coincides with the period for which annual accounts must be presented to shareholders.

The greatest benefit is derived from budgeting when:
1. It embraces the whole of the enterprise so that the management plan is stated in the form of a budgeted profit and loss statement, balance sheet, and funds statement.
2. It is used to assist managers in the control of business operations by showing them periodically – say monthly – the variances of actual from budgeted results for which they are responsible.

In circumstances when these two points apply, budgetary control may be said to operate. This implies that there is a formal routine laid down, possibly in a budget manual, to ensure that budgets are properly prepared in correct sequence; at the right time; in the proper form; whenever possible in quantity before being converted into monetary form; and are formally approved by the chief executive. After approval the budgeted profit and loss statement, balance sheet and funds statement may be termed the master budget.

Cash Budgeting

An important point to appreciate is that no plan of operations is complete unless sufficient cash is on hand at all times to meet obligations resulting from the plan. A proper balance between available and required cash is one of the most important requirements for sound financial management, indicating a clear need for a cash budget or forecast in some form. Only when all other budgets have been prepared is it feasible to produce a cash budget except in those very small concerns which operate only on a cash basis and therefore have no integrated budget system.

A quick method of budgeting cash at the end of a budget period is to budget all items in the balance sheet except cash, and the balancing figure will represent cash, a matter of deduction. However, this result should be supplemented by a month-by-month cash budget based on the receipts and payments dictated by the requirements of the other budgets of a business. A convenient layout is used on pages 77 and 78 in which an 'operating cash budget', showing a surplus or deficit of cash arising from current operations involving revenue rather than capital items is followed up by a 'financial budget', comprising all other receipts and payments, such as rent receivable, capital expenditure, taxation, etc.

A further method of budgeting for cash is to use the funds flow method demonstrated in Chapter 14.

A cash budget is seen to be a very important part of the budgetary planning procedure, for a shortage of cash might threaten the business with liquidation and on the other hand too much cash for any length of time is wasteful.

Comprehensive Example

The following example shows how in the budgetary control process one starts with the present financial position as shown by the balance sheet and by applying planned changes, can derive budgeted end-of-year statements.

Question

The Golden Hotel Co. Ltd. plan to enlarge a restaurant at a cost of £8,000 for kitchen plant and furnishings in order to make use of rooms not at present utilized. This money, to be funded from cash generated by the company, will be required to be paid out on 31st March, 1979, and a full year's depreciation (£800) will be charged in the year. Arrangements have been made with their bankers for the present overdraft facilities of up to £1,000 to be extended to £8,000 for twelve months from 1st April, 1979, after which time the maximum will revert to £1,000.

Budgetary control is operated by management and from the following details they require:

(*a*) Budgeted profit and loss statement for year 31st December, 1979
(*b*) Budgeted balance sheet as at 31st December, 1979
(*c*) Cash budget for months of January, February and March, 1979

Budget details:
  Budgeted Sales

	Jan. 79	Feb. 79	Mar. 79	Full year 1979
	£	£	£	£
Accommodation	3,600	3,600	4,000	50,000
Food	2,500	2,600	2,800	40,000
Liquor	4,500	4,700	5,000	60,000
Other sales	250	250	250	3,000
Budgeted other income	—	—	100	300

Note 1. 25% of accommodation sales are on credit and one month is the average period of credit.
  2. Total accommodation sales in December 1978 was £4,000.
  3. No credit is allowed for food, liquor and other sales.

Budgeted Credit Purchases (one month average)
  Food cost is 38% of sales revenue
  Liquor cost is 50% of sales revenue
  Other sales cost is 40% of sales revenue.

	Jan. 79	Feb. 79	Mar. 79	Full Year 1979
Budgeted Cash Costs	£	£	£	£
Wages and staff expenses	3,500	3,500	3,600	43,000
Departmental expenses	1,000	1,000	1,100	15,000
Heat, light and power	1,800	—	—	6,000
Administration	500	500	500	6,000
Advertising	2,000	2,000	1,000	5,000
Operational expenses	100	80	80	1,000
Rates and insurance	—	—	400	1,600
Repairs and maintenance	200	200	200	2,000
Other expenses	—	—	200	400

Balance Sheet Items
  Land and buildings valuation, stocks and debtors are budgeted to be the same figures at 31st December, 1979, as 1st January, 1979. Plant, furniture and equipment to be depreciated 10%. Creditors are to be allowed to increase by 10% in the year.

Staff Accommodation Expenses
  Wages and staff expenses shown under Budgeted Cash costs do not include staff accommodation expenses, budgeted at £1,000 for the year.

Balance Sheet as at 31st December, 1978

Employment of Capital

	Cost £	Cumulative Depreciation £	£
Fixed Assets			
Freehold land and buildings at valuation 1.12.66	80,000		80,000
Plant, furniture and equipment	22,000	9,000	13,000
	102,000	9,000	93,000
Current Assets			
Stocks at cost	3,500		
Debtors	1,000		
Cash at bank and in hand	12,000		
		16,500	
Current Liabilities			
Corporation Tax payable 1.1.79	7,000		
Creditors	4,200		
Proposed final dividends – gross	3,500		
		14,700	1,800
			94,800
Capital Employed			
Share Capital – 70,000 ordinary shares of £1 each authorized, issued and fully paid			70,000
Revenue Reserve			14,800
Corporation tax payable 1.1.80			10,000
			94,800

Solution

Budgeted Profit & Loss Statement for year ended 31st December, 1979

	Sales £	Cost of Sales £	Gross Profit £
Rooms	50,000	—	50,000
Food	40,000	15,200	24,800
Liquor	60,000	30,000	30,000
Other sales	3,000	1,200	1,800
	153,000	46,400	106,600

Deduct: Operating Expenses
  Wages and staff expenses   44,000
  Departmental expenses   15,000
  Heat, light and power   6,000
  Administration   6,000
  Advertising   5,000
  Operational expenses   1,000
                                            ———   77,000
                                                        ———————

                   HOTEL OPERATING PROFIT   29,600

Deduct: Property Expenses
  Rates and insurances   1,600
  Repairs and maintenance   2,000
  Depreciation   3,000
                                            ———   6,600
                                                        ———————
                                                        23,000
Add: Staff accommodation adjustment   1,000
                                                        ———————
             HOTEL NET OPERATING PROFIT   24,000

Deduct: Other Expenses/Income
  Expenses   400
  Income   300
                                            ——   100
                                                        ———————
                   NET PROFIT   23,900

  Provision for Corporation Tax   10,800
                                                        ———————
                                                        13,100
  Ordinary Dividends 10%   7,000
                                                        ———————
  Retained profit for the year   6,100
                                                        ═══════

Budgeted Balance Sheet as at 31st December, 1979

Employment of Capital	Cost £	Accumulated Depreciation £	£
Fixed Assets			
Freehold land and buildings			
at valuation 1.12.72	80,000	—	80,000
Plant, furniture and equipment	30,000	12,000	18,000
	110,000	12,000	98,000
Current Assets			
Stocks at cost		3,500	
Debtors		1,000	
Cash at bank and in hand (balancing figure)		17,110	
		21,610	
Current Liabilities			
Corporation tax payable 1.1.80	10,000		
Creditors	4,410		
Proposed final dividend – gross	3,500		
		17,910	3,700
			101,700
Capital Employed			
Share Capital – 70,000 ordinary shares of £1 each			
authorized, issued and fully paid			70,000
Revenue reserve balance 1.1.79		14,800	
Profit for the year retained		6,100	
			20,900
Corporation tax payable 1.1.81			10,800
			101,700

Operating Cash Budget – three months to 31st March, 1979

	January £	February £	March £
Receipts			
Sales: Rooms – credit	1,000	900	900
cash	2,700	2,700	3,000
Food	2,500	2,600	2,800
Liquor	4,500	4,700	5,000
Other Sales	250	250	250
	10,950	11,150	11,950

Payments

Food, liquor and others	4,200	3,300	3,440
Wages and staff expenses	3,500	3,500	3,600
Departmental expenses	1,000	1,000	1,100
Heat, light and power	1,800	—	—
Administration	500	500	500
Advertising	2,000	2,000	1,000
Operational expenses	100	80	80
Rates and insurance	—	—	400
Repairs and maintenance	200	200	200
	13,300	10,580	10,320
Operating cash surplus (deficit)	(2,350)	570	1,630

Financial Budget – 3 months to 31st March 1979

	January £	February £	March £
Opening cash balance/(overdraft)	12,000	(850)	(280)
Receipts			
Operating cash surplus/(deficit) (from operating cash budget)	(2,350)	570	1,630
Other income	—	—	100
	9,650	(280)	1,450
Payments			
Taxation	(7,000)	—	—
Ordinary dividend	(3,500)	—	—
Capital expenditure	—	—	(8,000)
Other expenses	—	—	(200)
	(10,500)	—	(8,200)
Closing cash balance/(overdraft)	(850)	(280)	(6,750)

Notes:
1. The monthly cash budget indicated that an overdraft of nearly £7,000 is expected early April, after which time a monthly operating cash surplus will reduce the overdraft. This budget has helped management to decide on the maximum overdraft facility required of £8,000.
2. The high cash balance at each year end has been accumulated to settle taxation and dividend payments in the first week of the new financial year.
3. The symbol ( ) is recognized as cash outflow.

Budgeting Principles

The amount of recorded detail involved will depend upon the size of the undertaking and generally speaking the larger business will require the more detailed, formal plans to aid communication and co-ordination between personnel. As with profit-motivated work of all kinds, the cost of producing desired results should be related to the value to the undertaking of the results obtained, whether the results be meals or figures to aid management. It is likely that detailed budgeting is not economic for the very small establishment, however an understanding of what budgets and budgetary control mean will enable the manager of the smaller unit to adapt the principles to his needs.

A basic principle of budgeting which should be carried out wherever feasible is that one should first establish physical quantity of work required to be done before calculating the revenue and cost. This is obviously necessary when starting a business and should be considered at annual budgeting time. This principle might be applied to sales turnover, cost of food, staff gearing for functions, maintenance and other work contracted out.

Another budgeting principle is that responsibility which is delegated to personnel should include responsibility for sales revenue and controllable costs, where this is appropriate, and that personnel should participate in preparing the budget of the functions or activity for which they accept responsibility.

The more complex the budgeting, the more it costs to run the system. As one wants value for money, each size of business will require a budgetary control system tailor-made to its own needs.

Budgetary Planning Procedures

The exhibits which follow are designed to illustrate budgetary planning procedures and in particular how budgets tie in with one another. With modifications the procedure could be applied to any size of hotel, but it must be borne in mind that a prerequisite is a well-classified and possibly coded set of accounts, which will provide current figures in the right form to assist in the preparation of budgets.

Sales revenue budget

This important budget sets the pattern for all other budgets and is influenced by planned work to be done, e.g. catering for numbers of customers, and the pricing policy of management. Sales revenue forecasts for food, liquor and other sales which precede the budget, are of only limited value until they are related to cost of goods sold and the resulting gross profit. With the same floor space available as the previous year, it is management's job to attract more customers to fill any surplus capacity and/or to alter the balance of space usage so that turnover, which attracts the greatest gross margin, is increased at the expense of lower gross margin work. The relative combination of the quantities of a variety of products that make up total sales is known as 'sales mix'. The alternative is to increase facilities, although care is needed to see that the extra demand does in fact exist, or is capable of being created by sales promotion.

Experience is all important in forecasting sales, although statistical method involving trend analysis may be found useful.

Food and liquor cost budget
Cost of food, liquor and other sales being variable costs are determined by multiplying turnover by the expected percentage of cost to turnover. For instance, if one plans for a food turnover of £40,000 and an expected food cost of 40% of turnover, then budgeted food cost will be £16,000 and gross margin £24,000 or 60% of turnover.

Wages and staff expenses budget
This cost budget is very important since it may amount to 30% of the value of sales turnover and is largely a controllable cost. For each budget centre there will be prepared a detailed budget, as Exhibit 6–2, and summarized to give total wages and staff expenses for the business, as Exhibit 6–3. Comparisons with the estimated actual costs for the current year will highlight any significant planned increases or decreases in costs.

Where variable costs are budgeted the level of activity to which they relate should be stated to assist in the control of such costs in the budget period.

The wages and staff expenses budgets illustrated provide for details which help towards more accurate estimating, but which may be omitted to save preparation time, so long as accuracy is not significantly affected.

Departmental expenses budget
Departmental expenses should be budgeted for budget centres with reference to the previous year's expenses, and more important in relation to the expectations of the budget period. For example, in Exhibit 6–4 there may have been £50 spent on protective clothing for the maintenance personnel late in the previous year and knowing that this clothing is almost new, only £20 may be budgeted for replacements in the budget year.

The budgeted departmental expenses may then be summarized as Exhibit 6–6, in preparation for inclusion in the budgeted profit and loss statement.

Budget centre budgets
The preparation of budgets for sales revenue, food and liquor costs, wages and staff expenses and departmental expenses coincides with the preparation of departmental or budget centre budgets. Budget centres are used for budgeting and may conveniently relate to departments, the essential point being that a person is responsible for the activities and financial results of a budget centre.

A cost centre is defined on page 140 and in many cases it may be regarded as a budget centre. In large establishments food and liquor budget centres will be further broken down into banqueting rooms and bars budgets. Chapter 10 deals with the classification of departments for accounting purposes.

Each budget centre budget (e.g. Exhibit 6–4) consists of any wages, staff expenses and departmental expenses which are capable of being directly related to the centre. Additionally, operated (revenue earning) centres will have budgeted revenue included and therefore budgeted profit. At this stage in the budget preparation there will be a profit (or loss) known variously as Hotel Operating Profit (Exhibit 10–2) or Responsibility Profit (Exhibit 6–7), revenue and costs so far being largely controllable.

Simply prepared budgets will be required for such remaining expenses as rates, insurance, depreciation, 'other expenses and income' and for capital expenditure.

Profit and loss budget
The revenue and expenses budgets need now to be amalgamated to form the profit and loss budget as Exhibit 6–7. Adjustments have to be made for staff accommodation expenses and other expenses and income before the budgeted net profit is arrived at.

It has been stated that forecasts precede budgets, and practice varies as to how many adjustments are made to a forecast profit and loss statement before the management is satisfied that the net profit is the right target for the next year. Forms such as those illustrated may be used for forecasting and are especially useful for budgets if they contain the previous year's estimated actual figures.

It must be appreciated that as the budgeting takes place before the end of that year an estimation of the expenses for the last month or two must be made and added to the latest actual figures available.

Budgeted balance sheet and cash budget
These two budgets complete the budgetary planning operation. However, a balance sheet needs to be prepared to show the expected position at the beginning of the budget period and, as explained, this would include estimated actual figures only. Further information to produce the budgeted balance sheet required, apart from budgets already mentioned, will be end of year stocks, debtors, creditors and any changes on capital account or on loan account.

The cash budget, as earlier explained, may be produced in a number of ways, depending upon whether or not a monthly figure is required.

Summary
Any commercial organization has a plan of operations and should have a profit target. Budgeting translates operating plans into accounting language and relates them to financial objectives. The operating plans originate in such areas as marketing, food production, personnel, accommodation, which constitute the non-financial aspects of management. These plans are then translated into revenues, costs, assets, and liabilities, which are summarized in the form of financial statements. A reasonable return on investment may be regarded as the overall financial goal and the evaluated plan must be seen to achieve this end. Budgeting and, in particular, budgetary control is potentially management's most useful and necessary tool.

The paper work involved in budgeting is to quantify and to integrate plans, an exercise which requires co-ordination of all personnel in any supervisory

Exhibit 6-2

GOLDEN HOTELS LTD.—WAGES AND STAFF EXPENSES BUDGET FOR 1980

BANQUETING MANAGER

Personnel	Fixed or Variable Cost	Rate	No. Persons	TOTAL	Salaries and Wages	O/time	Nat. Ins.	Staff Foods	Staff Acc.	Misc. Staff Expenses
				£	£	£	£	£	£	£
Manager	F									
Head waiter	F									
Head wine waiter	F									
Waiters (casual)	V									
Wine waiters (casual)	V									
Porters	F									
1980 BUDGET				10,000*						
1979 Estimated Actual										

REMARKS	Variable costs are based on Sales of £ for the year

Prepared by	Date	Approved by	Date

* Transferred to Banqueting Budget (not illustrated) also Wages and Staff Expenses Summary Budget.

Exhibit 6-3

GOLDEN HOTELS LTD.

WAGES AND STAFF EXPENSES SUMMARY BUDGET FOR 1980

| 1979 Estimated Actual | | BUDGET CENTRE | No. Persons | TOTAL | Salaries and Wages | O/time | Nat. Ins. | Staff Food | Staff Acc. | Misc. Staff Expenses |
No. Persons	TOTAL £			£	£	£	£	£	£	£
		Accommodation								
		General								
		Reception								
		Porterage								
		Linen room								
		Housekeeping								
		Food, Liquor & Tobacco								
		Kitchen								
		Restaurant								
		Banqueting rooms		10,000*						
		Bars								
		Cellars								
		Other Hotel Sales								
		Telephone								
		Cloaks								
		Administration								
		Gen. manager's office								
		Book-keeping								
		Operational expenses								
		Heat, light & power								
		Marketing								
		Repairs & maintenance		2,900†						
		TOTALS		60,000‡						

Prepared by	Date	Approved by	Date

REMARKS

* From Banqueting Budget   † From Repairs and Maintenance Budget   ‡ To Budgeted Profit & Loss Statement

Exhibit 6-4

REPAIRS AND MAINTENANCE BUDGET FOR 1980

1979 Estimated Actual £		1980 Budget £
	WAGES AND STAFF EXPENSES (Detailed on right)	2,900*
	Departmental Expenses	
	Hire charges	50
	Laundry	30
	Protective clothing	20
50	Building repairs (outside work)	200
		300†
		3,200

REMARKS

Prepared by	Date	Approved by	Date

* To Wages & Staff Expenses Summary Budget.
† To Departmental Summary Budget.

Exhibit 6-5

DETAILED WAGES AND STAFF EXPENSES BUDGET

WAGES & STAFF EXPENSES ANALYSIS	Rate	No. Persons	TOTAL £	S. & W. £	N.I. £	Staff Food £	Staff Acc. £
Manager							
Assistant							
1980 BUDGET			2,900				
1979 ESTIMATED ACTUAL							
REMARKS							

Exhibit 6-6

DEPARTMENTAL EXPENSES SUMMARY BUDGET FOR 1980

1979 Estimated Actual £	(Sample items only)	TOTAL £	Accommodation £	Food £	Liquor and Tobacco £	Other Hotel Sales £	Heat Light & Power £	Administration £	Marketing £	Operational £	Repairs and Maintenance £
	Banqueting expenses	x		x	x						
	Bar equipment replacement	x			x						
	Bar supplies	x			x						
	Building repairs (outside work)	x			x						200
	Contract cleaning	x	x	x							
	China & crockery replacement	x	x	x							
	Directories	x				x					
	Dry cleaning	x	x	x	x						
	Guest supplies	x	x	x	x						
	Hire charges	x	x	x	x						50
	Kitchen equipment replacement	x		x							30
	Laundry	x	x	x	x						
	Linen replacement	x	x	x	x						
	Menus & wine lists	x		x	x						
	Rental of T.V., etc.	x	x								
	Silverware replacement	x		x	x						
	Uniforms & protective clothing	x	x	x	x	x	x	x	x	x	20
	Vending machine expenses	x			x	x					
	1980 BUDGET	20,000*									300†

1979 ESTIMATED ACTUAL

* To Budgeted Profit & Loss Statement.
† From Repairs and Maintenance Budget. To Budgeted Profit & Loss Statement.

Exhibit 6-7   GOLDEN HOTELS—BUDGETED PROFIT AND LOSS STATEMENT FOR 1980

	1980 Sales £	Cost of Sales £	G.P. %	Wages and Staff Expenses £	Wages/Sales %	Departmental Expenses £	Profit (Loss) £	% of Sales	1979 Sales £	G.P. %	Wages %	Profit %	Profit £
OPERATED DEPARTMENTS													
Accommodation	x			x	x	x	x	x	x			x	x
Food	x	x	x	x	x	x	x	x	x	x		x	x
Liquor	x	x	x	x	x	x	x	x	x	x		x	x
Other sales	x	x	x	x	x	x	x	x	x	x		x	x
TOTAL	x	x	x	x	x	x	x	x	x	x		x	x
Operating Income	x						x	x	x			x	x
OPERATING PROFIT												x	x
Heat, light & power						x							
Administration				x	x	x					x		
Marketing						x					x		
Operational expenses						x							
Repairs & maintenance				2,900*	x	300*					x		
						20,000†	x	x				x	x
RESPONSIBILITY PROFIT							x	x				x	x
Rent, rates & insurance						x							x
Depreciation				60,000‡		x	x	x				x	x
NET PROFIT	x	x	x				x	x				x	x

Add: Staff accommodation
Other Expenses and Income   (−) or (+)

* From ... Maintenance Budget.   † From Departmental Summary Budget.   ‡ From Wages & Staff Expenses Budget.

capacity. Discussing and eventually agreeing plans leads to a smoother working relationship at the manager/supervisor level.

Continuous or Rolling Budget
Preparation of budgets once a year covering a 12-month period has been a natural development of financial accounting practice. It makes sense to plan operations for a financial year and to alter plans at the 6-monthly stage if necessary. However, towards the end of the financial year the next annual budget is being prepared and at this stage only about 2 months of plans remain. Recognizing the disadvantages of discreet 12-month plans, some enterprises now prepare continuous or rolling budgets to ensure that at the end of each month or quarter there is a full 12-month budget in front of their management. This is done by replacing the month or quarter just elapsed with a budget for a similar period added to what remains of the present budget.

Dynamic Forecasting
Dramatic and sudden changes in the economic scene caused by inflation and material shortages need quicker responses by business to such environmental factors. To meet these situations some companies now revise the whole of their 12-month forecast, every month, after taking into account events of the month just elapsed. They therefore have two forecasts going at the same time and naturally the revised one is the more accurate. The advantage is that marketing management are motivated into constantly looking into the future and finding ways of getting back on target as represented by their original forecast. Although the original forecast would have been linked with the budget, the revised forecast would not relate to the budget. Should the revised forecast become so different from the original one it would then be used to revise the 12-month budget.

Questions and Problems
6–1   Explain the terms 'budgeting' and 'budgetary control'.

6–2   What is a continuous budget?

6–3   'Too many department heads think that budgets represent a penny-pinching, negative brand of managerial pressure'. Cost Accounting, a managerial emphasis by Charles T. Horngren. Discuss this statement.

6–4   Why is the sales budget considered to be such an important element in budgetary planning?

6–5   Explain how an hotel housekeeping budget may be prepared and how it fits into the overall budgetary control plan.

6–6   Your catering organization has decided to introduce a comprehensive system of budgetary control. As a first step it has been agreed to form a budget committee, and you have been requested to prepare a report for your managing director on the functions of such a committee and who should serve on it.

6–7   You have recently been appointed manager of a medium sized hotel. The firm operates a very simple system of budgetary control, in that at the beginning of each quarter the managing director, without consultation, sets financial targets in respect of revenue and of expenditure for all departments of the hotel. In order to stimulate the director's interest in management techniques and aids, you have been passing over to him your copies of *The Caterer's Journal* each month. In one edition there appeared the undernoted flow chart depicting part of the budgeting process:

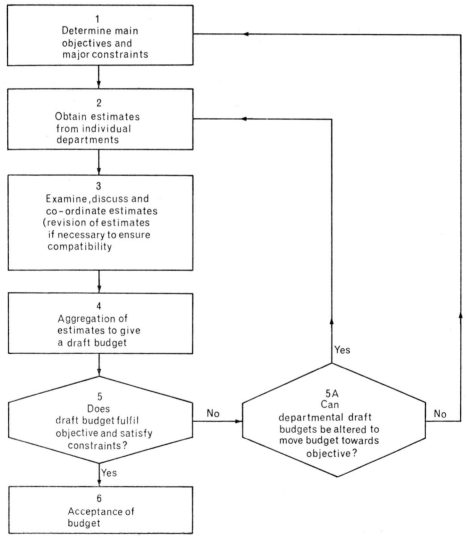

The managing director has asked you to prepare a memorandum commenting on each of the stages on the flow chart. Your comments should indicate whether you think each stage is necessary, and in so far as they appear to differ from the present system, what benefits could be expected to accrue if those stages with which you agree were introduced into the hotel.

6–8 Describe the organization and operation of a system of budgetary control, emphasizing the importance of human factors in enabling the system to be effective.

6–9 The Beach Restaurant is a seasonal licensed establishment. On 31st December, 1976, its balance sheet disclosed:

	£		£
Capital	50,000	Freehold property	30,000
Trade creditors	4,600	Equipment	12,500
		Stocks	9,200
		Debtors	2,000
		Cash at bank	900
	54,600		54,600

The following forecasts and information for the three months to 31st March, 1977, has been provided:

(a) Month	Sales of food & beverages	Purchases of food & beverages	Wages and other expenses	Dep'n of equipment
	£	£	£	£
Jan	16,000	9,000	8,000	200
Feb	20,000	10,000	9,000	200
Mar	24,000	8,000	11,000	200

(b) Gross profit on sales is an average of 60%.
(c) Half the sales are for cash, the balance being credit sales which are settled in the month after the date of transaction.
(d) All the purchases are on credit and suppliers are paid in the month after the date of the transaction.
(e) Wages and other expenses are paid out monthly in cash.
(f) A loan of £5,000 has been granted and will be received on 1st February. The annual interest rate is 12% to be paid half-yearly in arrears.
(g) On 1st February catering equipment is to be acquired, the price of which will be £7,500. The existing equipment that the new equipment is to replace is in the balance sheet at £1,500 and the supplier has agreed to accept it for a part exchange value of £1,000.

You are required to:
(a) prepare the monthly cash budget from January to March inclusive;
(b) calculate the closing stock value; and
(c) prepare a budgeted trading, profit and loss account for the quarter ending 31st March, 1977, and a budgeted balance sheet as at that date.

6–10   Draw up a monthly projected cash statement for the six months September 1975 to February 1976 from the following information:

			£		£
Payments:	Purchases	Sept.	14,000	Dec.	18,000
		Oct.	16,000	Jan.	22,000
		Nov.	18,000	Feb.	18,000
	Wages	Sept.	13,000	Dec.	15,000
		Oct.	13,500	Jan.	16,000
		Nov.	15,000	Feb.	13,500
	Expenses	Sept.	13,000	Dec.	15,000
		Oct.	14,000	Jan.	15,500
		Nov.	14,500	Feb.	14,000
Income from Sales:		Sept.	53,000	Dec.	61,000
		Oct.	34,000	Jan.	65,000
		Nov.	32,000	Feb.	70,000

Other items:	Expenditure on Capital equipment	Sept.	10,000
		Nov.	10,000
		Jan.	15,000
	Sale of equipment	Dec.	5,000
	Sale of land	Jan.	10,000
	Dividend from subsidiary	{ Dec.	3,000
	companies	{ Feb.	5,000
	Tax payment due	Feb.	6,000

The projected cash balance at the beginning of September is £3,000. It is planned to pay out a dividend of £26,000 in January.

Make brief comments on the position disclosed.

6–11   D. Server Ltd. intends to commence business as a caterer on the 1st January, 1977. Initial requirements are expected to be fittings and equipment £500, and stocks £4,500. Meals are expected to be sold at $33\frac{1}{3}\%$ above cost. Expected sales are £3,000 per month for the first two months and £4,000 per month for the remaining ten months. Three months' credit will be allowed on sales, and one month's credit is expected from suppliers of food and beverages and equipment. Monthly expenses paid out in cash will be £800. This does not include exceptional expense items of £100 which will be paid in February and August. Food and beverage stock will be replaced in full the month after they are used. You are required to:

    (*a*) estimate the capital requirements of D. Server Ltd. with the aid of a cash budget for 1977. (Assume that an initial amount of £9,000 can be raised in the form of ordinary share capital, and any additional funds can be obtained in the form of a bank overdraft.)

    (*b*) prepare a projected profit statement and balance sheet for 1977. (Fittings and equipment depreciation is to be calculated at 20% per annum, and taxation at 50% of net profit.)

    (*c*) comment on the projected results for 1977. (The managing director of D. Server Ltd. considers that a satisfactory return on a capital is 18% before interest and taxation.)

Further Reading

1. Cox, B. and Hewgill, J. C. R., *Management Accounting in Inflationary Conditions*, I.C.M.A.
2. Boardman, R. D., *Hotel and Catering, Costing and Budgets*, Heinemann; chapters 16 & 17.
3. Bishop, E. B., Mackay, A. D., Chambers, A., Sizer, J., *Aspects of Corporate Planning*, I.C.M.A.
4. Horngren, C. T., *Cost Accounting, A Managerial Emphasis*, Prentice-Hall; chapter 5.
5. Clarkson, G. P. and Elliot, B. J., *Managing Money and Finance*, Gower Press; chapter 3.

CHAPTER SEVEN

BUDGETARY CONTROL

HAVING set a budget for a 12-month period management take steps to monitor progress of actual operations and the resulting revenues and costs. The publications *A Standard System of Hotel Accounting* and *A Standard System of Catering Accounting* give excellent assistance to those looking for basic accounting systems to help them control their revenues and costs. These works will be referred to in detail in Chapter 10. The intention here is to explain briefly proved control mechanisms, some included in the standard systems, others going beyond yet contained within the framework laid down. The approach here is to show firstly how gross profit can be monitored and variances calculated for control purposes. This entails studying sales and the cost of sales in some detail. Wages and expenses will then be dealt with and related to the standard system.

Control may be said to be the guidance of the internal operations of the business towards producing the most satisfactory profit at the lowest cost, and should be based on sound planning. Profit, being influenced by volume, selling price and cost, is controlled by marketing management who are responsible for revenue, and the entire management team who incur and control costs.

Cost Control Principles

There is no question that costs have to be controlled in a business, for it is natural that without some control mechanism in force, costs would surely rise. It is in the nature of things to spend money if no restraint is put on money available. The problem arises in a business as to the method used to control cost, and the cost of running the cost control system. Undoubtedly, there comes a time when the cost control system outweighs the benefits derived therefrom, so that a compromise usually results. However, the commonsense approach usually prevails and this dictates:

(a) It is a waste of effort to attempt to control costs which defy control. Effort should be put to determine whether the service for which the cost is incurred is necessary and, if so, whether alternative and cheaper means are available for supplying the service.

(b) Of the costs which are controllable, those constituting the highest cost should receive most attention from the control point of view.

In the first category such costs as local rates, maintenance, insurance and telephone rental are included and may be termed 'fixed costs' as they tend to remain unaffected by changes in turnover.

In the hotel and catering industry, the costs which represent the highest percentage of sales are cost of food, liquor and tobacco. It is also true that these costs are about the only true 'variable cost' of a business and as such are susceptible to fairly close control.

It is not surprising, therefore, that costs of food, liquor and tobacco are generally well controlled in hotels and restaurants. This is achieved by relating cost of food as a percentage to the sales revenue and comparing the percentage with past performance or with a budget.

Gross Profit Control

(a) Exhibit 7–1
The simplest of control statements is Exhibit 7–1. It can be seen that planned gross profit has fallen by £340 and that food costs have risen more than the revenue. It might be inferred that food has cost an extra £440 only because it should stay at 50% of sales (£3,300), but this will be seen to be inaccurate. More information is needed to obtain better control figures.

Exhibit 7–1

Simple Control Statement

No. dishes	Budget 3,000		Actual 2,865	
	£	%	£	%
Sales	6,400	100	6,600	100
Food cost	3,200	50	3,740	57
Gross profit	3,200	50	2,860	43

How far a business is prepared to systematically analyse the difference between actual and budget depends very much on the size of turnover. A small restaurateur may be content with the above summary for it would act more as a check on what he expected the results to be. However, the manager of a large restaurant with 50 times the turnover would require more detail to help him pinpoint factors causing the adverse position.

(b) Exhibit 7–2
Additional information has been obtained and inserted into a control statement. As just noted the difference in the gross profits of the 'simple control statement' (Exhibit 7–1) is £340 and it is this figure that features prominently in this more complex statement. The extra information used is the make up of the budget consisting of two different dishes A and B and the actual number of dishes served in the period.

Exhibit 7–2

GROSS PROFIT CONTROL STATEMENT (FOOD)

Dish category	Original Budget[1]						Control Budget[2]						Actual		Variances
	A 1,000	%	B 2,000	%	Total 3,000	%	A 1,643	%	B 1,222	%	Total 2,865	%	Total 2,865	%	£
No. dishes															
	£		£		£		£		£		£		£		
Sales revenue	2,800	100	3,600	100	6,400	100	4,600	100	2,200	100	6,800	100	6,600	100	(200)
Food cost	1,200	43	2,000	56	3,200	50	1,972	43	1,222	56	3,194	47	3,740	57	(546)
Gross profit	1,600	57	1,600	44	3,200	50	2,628	57	978	44	3,606	53	2,860	43	(746)

£406   £(746)

£(340)

Notes:

Symbol ( ) = adverse variance, otherwise variances are favourable

Control budget food costs are derived from food cost % to 2 decimal places viz. 42·86% (A)

Summary:

	£
Sales margin volume variance	406
Sales margin price variance	(200)
Food cost variance	(546)
Total Gross Profit Variance	(340)

[1]Sometimes referred to as a 'fixed budget'

[2]Sometimes referred to as a 'flexible budget'.

The control budget has been derived in the following manner by bearing in mind a very important cost control principle which states 'to assess whether a cost in a period is acceptable without further investigation it should be compared with the cost that was expected in order to produce actual output'. Considering the control budget of A, a revenue of £4,600 should have come from 1,643 dishes. The calculation is either 1,643 × £2·80 (dish price) or £2,800 × $\frac{1,643}{1,000}$. Likewise food cost should rise with this large rise in sales, to the extent of £1,972, calculated 43% of £4,600 or 1,643 × £1·20 (dish cost). Adding the control budgets of A and B gives figures management would expect to see because of the favourable sales achievement in the period. All other things being equal there should be extra gross profit of £406 as shown in the statement as a favourable volume variance because of increased activity.

The control budget indicates the revenue and food cost management was looking for at the end of the period. But a comparison with actual recordings in the accounts shows that revenue was £200 short and food cost £546 too much. These two variances together with the volume variance of £406 reconcile with the total difference of £340.

Food Cost Variances
To find out the reasons for the extra food cost, standard food prices and usages need to be introduced and an enterprise using 'Standard food costing' would have this information available. Standard costing is the name given to the technique whereby standard costs are predetermined and subsequently compared with the actual recorded costs. The difference between the standard cost of meals or dishes in a period, and the actual cost, is known as the cost variance which can be broken down into its component parts of usage variance and price variance. These may be calculated as follows:

Usage variance = Standard price (Standard quantity – actual quantity)
Price variance = Actual quantity (Standard price – actual price)

The following figures are made available so that these variances may be calculated:

Actual Data
Dishes A and B consist of food Y and Z respectively and the standard food cost of each dish is:
  A : 500 grammes of Y @ £2·40 per kilo = £1·20
  B : 500 grammes of Z @ £2·00 per kilo = £1·00
In the period when 1,643 dishes of A and 1,222 dishes of B were served the following food was used:
  800 kilos of Y @ £2·80 per kilo
  625 kilos of Z @ £2·40 per kilo

For calculation purposes the following method is recommended:
(a) Standard food quantity @ standard price } Usage variance
(b) Actual food quantity @ standard price }
(c) Actual food quantity @ actual price } Price variance

Applying this procedure to the example:

	Meal A – Food Y	£	£ Variance
(a)	1,643 dishes × 500 grammes = 821·5 kilos @ £2·40 = 1,972		52 Usage
(b)	800 kilos @ £2·40 = 1,920		
(c)	800 kilos @ £2·80 = 2,240		(320) Price

Total food cost variance   (a − c)   =   (268)

Variances for B calculated in similar fashion added to A variances may be summarized:

	A	B	Total
	£	£	£
Usage variances	52	(28)	24
Price variances	(320)	(250)	(570)
	(268)	(278)	(546)

The food cost adverse variance of £546 initially discovered in the 'Gross Profit Control Statement' has now been shown to have been caused by price rises of £570 and the kitchen usage has been favourable to the extent of £24.

More details concerning standard costing may be found in *A Standard System of Catering Accounting*.

Sales Margin Variances

Preparation of the gross profit control statement automatically highlighted that sales revenue was short of end-of-period expectations by £200 after allowing for an extra £406 gross profit from increased activity. Without doubt the £200 fall is due to average selling prices being lower than planned. In those establishments where sales mix is important to plan and control, it is possible to get some idea of the effect changes in sales mix have on gross profit. The following method is used by sales-orientated firms in other industries and the variances derived are an invaluable aid to marketing management. The object is to break down the volume variance into mix variance and residual volume variance (or quantity variance). To do this it is assumed that overall gross profit % in the budget has been maintained (with costs and selling prices unchanged). If this % has improved this must be a reflection of a more profitable sales mix. From the gross profit control statement it can be seen by inspection that the sales mix is favourable compared with the original budget, and the following method simply quantifies it. As in the control budget, standard dish prices and costs are assumed.

(a) Actual total sales × actual gross profit %
(b) Actual total sales × budgeted gross profit %   } Mix variance

(c) Budgeted total sales × budgeted gross profit % } Quantity variance

Applying this to the example, it will be seen that by referring to the gross profit control statement, the two budgeted gross profits can be lifted from the statement and one calculation is needed to analyse the difference between them.

		£	£	Variances
(a) £6,800 × 53·03%	=	3,606 ⎫	206	Mix
(b) £6,800 × 50%	=	3,400 ⎬		
(c) £6,400 × 50%	=	3,200 ⎭	200	Quantity
Total sales margin Volume variance		406		

Terms used are not important but sales margin mix, quantity and volume may be used to show that the margin or gross profit is affected by sales mix, quantity and volume.

A full reconciliation statement can now be prepared as follows:

Statement reconciling budgeted with actual gross profit

	£	£
Budgeted gross profit		3,200
Apply sales margin variances		
Price	(200)	
Quantity	200	
Mix	206	206
		3,406
Apply food cost variances		
Price	(570)	
Usage	24	(546)
Actual gross profit		2,860

Control of Wages and Expenses

Food and liquor costs are tightly controlled because of their significance and of being susceptible to control. Most other costs are either semi-variable or fixed and not so easily controlled. However, they do need to be systematically controlled and one way is to use a 'Flexible Budget'. This (see Exhibit 7–3) is equivalent to the 'Control Budget' as used in the gross profit control statement for it includes a column headed 'Flexible Budget' designed to reflect what cost was expected in the period bearing in mind the sales achieved. It can be seen that semi-variable expenses have been adjusted to take account of the rise in sales, leaving variances due to price or usage of the item, which require separate explanations. As with food control statements the difference between the original budget and the control or flexible budget is a volume variance caused entirely by sales activity change.

Recommended statements in the standard accounting systems can be adapted to accept this extra control measure where considered appropriate.

A.F.M./2—G

Exhibit 7-3

ROOM DEPARTMENT COST CONTROL STATEMENT
(6 months ended ....)

	Cost Class	(1) Fixed Budget		(2) Flexible Budget		(3) Actual		(4) Variance (Col. 3−2)	(5) Remarks
		£	%	£	%	£	%	£	Increased turnover caused by......
Guest accommodation		20,000		22,000		22,000			
Room Hire		1,000		1,100		1,100			
TOTAL SALES		21,000		23,100		23,100			
Gross Pay									
N.I.									
Holiday Pay									
Staff Meals									
Staff accommodation									
TOTAL WAGE & STAFF COST	S.V.	7,000		7,100		7,100		—	
NET MARGIN		14,000		16,000		16,000		—	
Department supplies	S.V.	1,500		1,600		1,700		(100)	Minor equip. for rooms
Flowers & decorations	F.	300		300		320		(20)	Price increase
Magazines & periodicals	F.	100		100		90		10	
Printing & Stationery	S.V.	400		430		420		10	
Laundry & dry cleaning charges	S.V.	700		750		800		(50)	Under est. in quantity of dry cleaning
Cleaning Contracts	F.	500		500		500		—	
Linen	S.V.	100		105		105		—	
Uniforms	S.V.	200		200		200		—	
Utensils	F.	200		200		200		—	
TOTAL ALLOCATED EXPENSE		4,000		4,185		4,335		(150)	
DEPARTMENTAL OPERATING PROFIT		10,000		11,815		11,665		(150)	

SUMMARY	£
Profit variance due to volume (Col. 2−1)	1,815
Profit variance due to price/usage (Col. 3−2)	(150)
TOTAL PROFIT VARIANCE FROM BUDGET (Col. 3−1)	1,665

By admitting that certain costs must rise in sympathy with activity, due allowance is given for these and attention is directed to changes which were not foreseen either because of difficulty in determining cost behaviour. change in price, or because of poor cost control.

It should be noted that the flexible budget costs are not part of the double entry accounting system but are memorandum figures prepared as and when required. It is necessary, however, to record information on cost behaviour to enable reasonably accurate flexible budgets to be prepared and also to provide a basis for the annual budget.

Responsibility Accounting

Cost control is best achieved when personnel accept responsibility for costs under their control even if they do not have the 100% control over some costs that they would like.

Routine reports may be constructed to show separately those costs which the recipient is required to control, and those he cannot control (non-controllable costs). The organization must be divided into responsibility centres – defined as an organizational unit having a single head accountable for activities of the unit. A budget centre often coincides with a responsibility centre.

A responsibility accounting system is operated within the budgetary control system and its requirements are:

(*a*) the individual in charge is held to be responsible for the activities within his jurisdiction, and the effort used in attaining his objectives is to be measured in terms of Controllable and Non-Controllable costs.

(*b*) The organization chart of the firm, supported by a schedule of cost responsibilities is the basis on which reports are prepared and recognition of controllable and non-controllable costs and revenue made.

Exhibit 7–4 gives an example

Exhibit 7–4

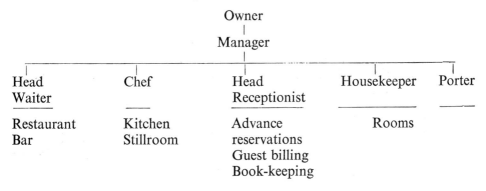

Hotel Organization Chart (Extract)

Schedule of Cost Responsibilities (Extract)

	Head Waiter	*Manager*	*Owner*
Wages of waiters	C	C	C
Flowers	C	C	C
Laundry	C	C	C
Breakages	C	C	C
Music	N/C	C	C
Repairs	N/C	C	C
Stationery	N/C	N/C	C
Cleaning Contract	N/C	N/C	C

C = Controllable
N/C = Non-controllable

All costs are controllable by the proprietor in the sense that he has the choice to incur them in the first instance.

Human Relations Aspects of Cost Control

Human factors involved in budgetary control are generally more difficult to deal with than the technical matters of quantifying budgets and preparing control statements. Far from motivating personnel to take the right decision in the company's interest, an ill-conceived budget and budgetary control system can have the opposite effect. The very name 'budget' may be associated with imposition, dictation from top management, and niggardly allowances. If such attitudes are not eliminated by proper education at the start of a budget programme, and good communications in the budget operation, then the objective of improved profit may not be attained.

A large percentage of supervisors in industry generally regard budgetary control as having an important impact on performance of their activity. If this influence is in the wrong direction then serious financial consequences could occur. Budgetary control may not be making a full contribution if supervisors see the budget as being too rigid in operation or, on the other hand, too often altered, or if they find performance reports badly presented to them. Since supervisors are basically concerned with the present and with handling immediate problems, budget figures may be ignored in order to solve pressing difficulties.

Without doubt, management faces many problems when installing a budgetary control system not the least being the human problems. However, the right attitude should be that budgetary control is necessary and profitable although some imperfections in the system are inevitable. A balance must be struck between perfecting a system at great cost rendering it uneconomic, and getting value for money from a less costly system.

Management by Objectives (M.B.O.)

This is defined[1] as 'a technique under which targets are fixed as a basis for achieving greater effectiveness throughout the whole of an organization or

[1]*Glossary of Management Techniques*, published by H.M.S.O.

part of an organization'. It differs from budgetary control in two major ways in that targets may be non-financial such as a percentage increase in output or sales, and it may be applied to only a part of the organization.

It is claimed that since managers participate in setting their own objectives a system of self-control replaces one of imposed control. In general M.B.O. is concerned with the individual more so than is budgetary control and ideally there should be close links between the operation of both techniques.

Divisional Performance

If a manager of a subsidiary company, division or operating unit has control over costs and revenue, the unit may be regarded as a profit centre, and the manager's performance measured in financial terms. With an increasing amount of delegated responsibility being placed on managers' shoulders it is important to measure their contribution to corporate profit. No standard measure is available although where feasible some relationship to capital employed would appear appropriate, the obvious method being a target return on investment incurred by the unit of say 50% increase over the next three years. A method recommended by Professor David Solomons is a residual profit target, that is the profit remaining after deducting the cost of capital invested in the unit. Both these methods involve determining the capital employed of a unit, say a large hotel, but the assessment of this figure is not a simple matter, for each year the market value of the hotel rises and a higher profit is required to maintain the same return on capital as before.

Questions and Problems

7–1 What is the basic limitation of an original/fixed budget when it comes to control of trading activities?

7–2 What is a control/flexible budget and how might it be applied to an hotel or catering organization?

7–3 'There is only one kind of budget which is any use for monitoring purposes and that is a control/flexible budget'.
You are required to:
    (a) comment on this quotation;
    (b) discuss the factors which you would take into account in deciding the volume base e.g. meals, sales, revenue etc., you would select for measuring changes in activity; and
    (c) state what factors, other than the changes in the level of activity, would cause costs to vary.

7–4 Explain, in brief, the following terms:
    (a) standard cost   (d) food usage variance
    (b) standard price   (e) sales margin variance
    (c) food price variance   (f) sales mix variance

7–5   Select a particular type of hotel or catering establishment and suggest which departments, and who within the departments, are concerned with setting standards.

7–6   Enumerate the likely causes of food cost variances and sales margin variances.

7–7   Explain the relationship between the food price variance and the food usage variance. Is it feasible for a favourable result achieved from one variance to contribute to an adverse result in another variance?

7–8   Distinguish between controllable and non-controllable costs giving examples of each.

7–9   Explain what you understand by 'responsibility accounting'.

7–10 The following information relates to the Food and Beverage Budget of the Berkshire Banqueting Suite for 1st quarter of 1977:

Budgeted number of meals	Menu A	3,000
	Menu B	4,000
	Menu C	5,000
Budgeted selling prices per meal	Menu A	£4
	Menu B	£5
	Menu C	£3
Budgeted food cost per meal	Menu A	40%
	Menu B	30%
	Menu C	50%

Semi-variable cost behaviour attributable to various levels of activity are estimated to be:
  £25 per 100 meals from   100– 4,000
  £20 per 100 meals from 4,001– 8,000
  £15 per 100 meals from 8,001–12,000
Fixed costs for the quarter are £20,000. Budgeted activity is 60% of capacity.
Actual results were:

Number of meals sold (sales mix)	Menu A	12%
	Menu B	40%
	Menu C	48%

Food cost £15,700
Semi-variable costs £2,100
Activity was 50% of capacity at budgeted selling prices.
You are required to prepare a cost control statement for 1st quarter, 1977, to include:
   (a) an original/fixed budget;
   (b) a control/flexible budget;

(c) actual results; and
(d) variances
Comment on the results you have produced.

7–11 The following is a standard dish cost card for 20 portions of Crêpes au Disaster:

			£		£
2 litres	milk	@	0·10 litre		
½ kilo	flour	@	0·18 kilo		
4	eggs	@	0·05 each		
450 gms	castor sugar	@	0·26 kilo		
4	lemons	@	0·07 each		

Total Cost

During the period the following occurred in respect of Crêpes au Disaster:

Actual number of covers served 1,600

Ingredients	Actual Usage	Actual Price
milk	150 litres	0·10 litre
flour	45 kilos	0·16 kilo
eggs	360	0·06 each
castor sugar	30 kilos	0·28 kilo
lemons	320	0·06 each

You are required to:

(a) complete the standard dish cost card;
(b) calculate the total variances (not individual ingredient variances) for:
    (i) food usage;
    (ii) food price; and
    (iii) total food cost; and
(c) prepare a statement reconciling the standard food cost with actual food cost.

7-12 A medium sized provincial restaurant operates a system of standard food costing. From the information given below, you are required to:

(a) calculate the ingredient cost variances;
(b) calculate the sales margin variances; and
(c) reconcile the restaurant's budgeted and actual gross profit.

Number of covers budgeted was 12,000. The actual number of covers realized was 10,800 and the sales achieved from these were £11,400. The average spending power was expected to be £1·05 per head.

The standard cost per dish is:

Standard Dish Cost Card	
Ingredients	£
A 500 gms. @ £0·80 per kilo	0·40
B 125 gms. @ £1·20 per kilo	0·15
Total food cost per portion	0·55

Actual figures relating to the ingredients were:

Ingredient	Food Used kilo	Food price per kilo £
A	5,400	0·70
B	1,500	1·30

Further Reading

1. Burke, W. L., and Smyth, E. B., *Accounting for Management*, Sweet and Maxwell; chapters 3 and 4.
2. Horngren, C. T., *Cost Accounting, A managerial emphasis*, Prentice-Hall; chapters 8 and 9.
3. *A Standard System of Catering Accounting*, Hotel and Catering E.D.C., H.M.S.O.

CHAPTER EIGHT

COST – PROFIT – VOLUME ANALYSIS

BEFORE finalizing a profit plan, account should be taken of feasible alternative plans or forecasts to ensure that the best planned use is made of available resources. Alternative plans might consider such factors as pricing policy, food supply and prices, advertising, and standards for portion control.

When additional capital is included in a forecast, a number of methods might be used to assess the profitability of the investment, ranging from average rate of return to the more elaborate net present value method using the discounted cash flow technique. This chapter will deal only with the planning of profit from existing resources, leaving the subject of appraising further investment to be dealt with separately in Chapter 15.

Profit Relative to Turnover

Planning improvements in profit is not merely an exercise in figure-work: it requires practical, feasible ideas to come from management so that there is something to quantify in financial terms. One factor in the industry crying out for improvement, is the percentage capacity or occupancy of existing establishments, and fortunately there is evidence that the marketing minded manager in particular is achieving success in this area. Fortes for instance took over an hotel and within 3 years were able to double the turnover and treble the profit with negligible extra investment, and there was still a large gap between actual and potential turnover which they worked on and reduced.

Considering that an extra £1½ million turnover from an hotel group could well contribute more than £½ million extra profit without additional facilities and that when an hotel moves from 70% to 80% occupancy the additional turnover is almost completely extra profit it can be seen how important it is to acquire an understanding of how changes in level of activity such as turnover affects profit. This understanding can come from simple examples illustrated by charts.

The first example is of a stallholder at a market, similar in many ways to the restaurant but relieved of all the complication of food production and variety of dishes.

The stall has been hired for £12 covering a short period when it is planned to sell articles at £5 each which have cost £3 on a sale or return basis. The target is to sell all 12 articles that are available.

Analysis of costs involved in the enterprise shows two clear categories, namely a fixed or period cost of £12 which has to be paid regardless of how many articles are sold and a variable cost of £3 which varies in total directly with changes in sales level. No other costs are incurred.

Break-even Chart

To obtain a picture of all possible results taking into account the constraints of cost, selling price and maximum quantity, the break-even chart shown in Exhibit 8–1 has been prepared. This form of chart clearly portrays the quantitative factors of the situation, indicating for instance that when six articles have been sold or £30 cash received from sales any possibility of a loss has passed, and any further sales will provide a profit. Profit or loss expected at any sales level can be found by measuring the distance between revenue and total cost against the vertical scales, for example a profit of £8 is measured at the 10 unit level.

Exhibit 8–1

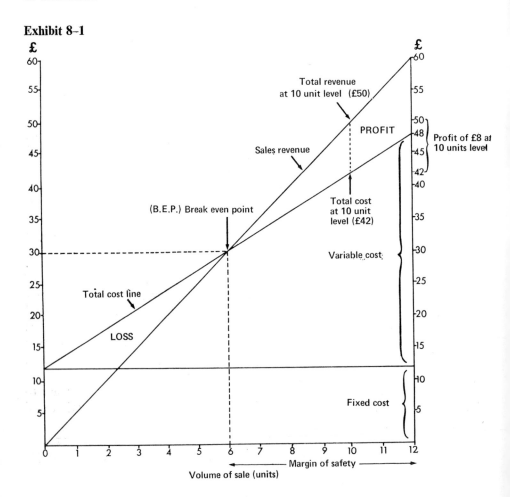

Exhibit 8–1a

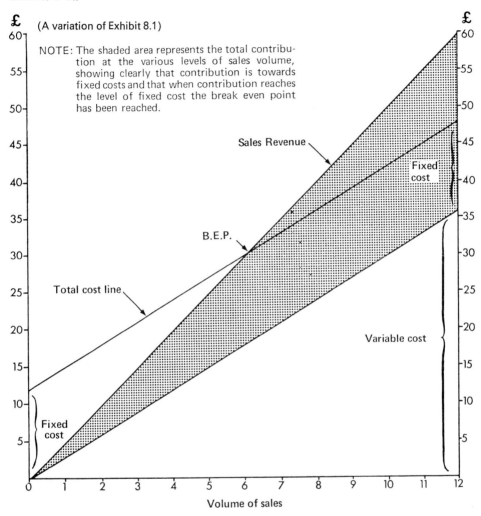

(A variation of Exhibit 8.1)

NOTE: The shaded area represents the total contribution at the various levels of sales volume, showing clearly that contribution is towards fixed costs and that when contribution reaches the level of fixed cost the break even point has been reached.

Volume of sales

DRAWING A BREAK-EVEN CHART (EXHIBIT 8–1)

1. Calculate values of maximum sales revenue and maximum activity, activity being measured in units, covers, hours, etc.
2. Determine X (horizontal) and Y (vertical) scales taking into account:
   (*a*) Y scale represents £s
   (*b*) X scale represents activity
   (*c*) maximum sales and activity
   (*d*) the larger the scale the more accurate will be results
   (*e*) wherever possible multiples of 5 or 2 in the scale
   (*f*) a chart may cover 1 month, 3 months or 1 year according to the problem.

3. Draw in X line and two Y lines, one from 0 and one from maximum X value, inserting scales, bottom left being 0.
4. Mark off maximum sales value on right hand Y line and join up to 0 with a straight line. This represents sales revenue.
5. On left and right hand Y mark off fixed cost and join points with a line parallel to base line.
6. Inserting variable costs above the fixed cost will give a line representing total cost. Two points needed for total cost line is the fixed cost point on left hand Y and total cost point at maximum activity (a calculation is needed here).
7. Break-even point is where total cost line cuts sales revenue.
8. A vertical dotted line from break-even point (B.E.P.) touches X at activity B.E.P.
9. A horizontal dotted line from B.E.P. to left hand Y shows sales turnover at B.E.P.

The B.E.P., at the level where total revenue equals total cost, can be stated in any of the following terms:

(a) Six units of sale (on horizontal line X)
(b) 50% maximum capacity (on horizontal line X)
(c) £30 turnover (on vertical line Y)

The 'Margin of Safety' is the complement of the break-even point, that is the drop in sales from maximum capacity before a loss is made, for instance 6 units in this case. Therefore B.E.P. + Margin of Safety = 100%. The same information extracted from this statement can be shown in a table (Exhibit 8–2) and the two presentations compared, for they are merely variations in form.

Exhibit 8–2

STATEMENT OF POSSIBLE RESULTS
TOTAL COST APPROACH

1 Number sold	2 Fixed cost	3 Variable cost (Col. 1 × £3)	4 Total cost (Col. 2+3)	5 Sales revenue (Col. 1 × £5)	6 Profit/(Loss) (Col. 5−4)
	£	£	£	£	£
0	12	0	12	0	(12)
1	12	3	15	5	(10)
2	12	6	18	10	(8)
3	12	9	21	15	(6)
4	12	12	24	20	(4)
5	12	15	27	25	(2)
6	12	18	30	30	0
7	12	21	33	35	2
8	12	24	36	40	4
9	12	27	39	45	6
10	12	30	42	50	8
11	12	33	45	55	10
12	12	36	48	60	12

Contribution

An important concept in profit planning is the term 'contribution' which is the sales revenue less variable cost. The stallholder receives a contribution of £2 for each article sold (£5–£3). A period when no sales were made at all would involve him in £12 loss (stall hire), but every article sold would contribute £2 towards reducing this loss, until the £12 had been balanced by contributions.

Exhibit 8–3 shows this approach in table form. It can be seen that articles sold 'contribute' towards the fixed cost, and when this has been 'recovered' all additional contributions represent profit, e.g. at 7 unit level profit = 1 contribution @ £2. Where the only significant variable cost is food, liquor, etc., then for practical purposes, contribution may be regarded as gross profit.

Exhibit 8–3

STATEMENT OF POSSIBLE RESULTS
CONTRIBUTION APPROACH

1	2	3	4	5	6	7	8
Number sold	Sales revenue (Col. 1 × £5)	Variable cost (Col. 1 × £3)	Contribution (Col. 2 – 3)	Fixed cost	Loss (Col. 4 – 5)	Profit (Col. 4 – 5) or (Col. 8 × £2)	Units sold above B.E.P. of 6
	£	£	£	£	£	£	
0	0	0	0	12	(12)		
1	5	3	2	12	(10)		
2	10	6	4	12	(8)		
3	15	9	6	12	(6)		
4	20	12	8	12	(4)		
5	25	15	10	12	(2)		
6	30	18	12	12		0	
7	35	21	14	12		2	1
8	40	24	16	12		4	2
9	45	27	18	12		6	3
10	50	30	20	12		8	4
11	55	33	22	12		10	5
12	60	36	24	12		12	6

Profit-Volume Chart

The profit-volume chart in Exhibit 8–4 is drawn to show this characteristic of the contribution. Two clear advantages can be claimed for this chart compared with the break-even chart:

(a) Profit or loss at any level can be read off more easily.

(b) Because of its simplicity in appearance, variations in contribution and fixed cost can be shown on one chart.

Exhibit 8–4

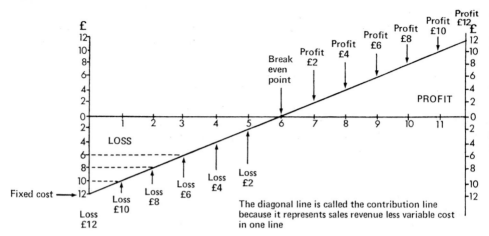

The diagonal line is called the contribution line because it represents sales revenue less variable cost in one line

Instructions for preparation of the profit-volume chart are as follows:

1. Calculate profit at maximum sales level. This added to the fixed cost is the maximum value of the vertical (Y) line.
2. Draw the vertical line to scale and insert 0 value so that above it represents profit and below it fixed cost.
3. Draw in the horizontal (X) line to a scale to represent sales units.
4. The 'contribution' line starts at the fixed cost point on the vertical line and needs one more point to fix its position. This point can be either the break-even point or the profit at any particular sales level, and each involves calculation.
5. The fixed cost is joined to, say, the B.E.P. and the profit graph is completed.

Should the stallholder be faced with a £16 charge for the period the profit volume chart representing this situation – Exhibit 8–5 indicates a break-even point of 8 units and a profit of £8 if all 12 articles were sold.

Exhibit 8–5

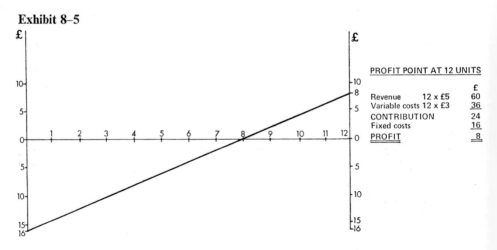

PROFIT POINT AT 12 UNITS

		£
Revenue	12 x £5	60
Variable costs	12 x £3	36
CONTRIBUTION		24
Fixed costs		16
PROFIT		8

If he then increased his selling price to £5·5 to counter the increased fixed cost, with cost remaining at £3 each a further chart – Exhibit 8–6 shows a break-even point of 7 (6·4) and a profit of £14 if all 12 articles were sold.

Exhibit 8–6

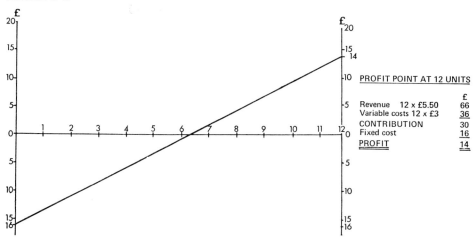

PROFIT POINT AT 12 UNITS

		£
Revenue	12 x £5.50	66
Variable costs	12 x £3	36
CONTRIBUTION		30
Fixed cost		16
PROFIT		14

All three situations may be shown on a single chart (Exhibit 8–7) facilitating useful comparisons. Comparing the 3rd situation with the 1st he would improve profit by £2 if he sells all 12, but if business were poor he would be £1 out of pocket instead of breaking even, if only 6 were sold. From Exhibit 8–4 it can be seen that the calculation of break-even point in units is:

Total fixed cost for period ÷ contribution per unit

Using the original figures in Exhibit 8–1 the break-even point is calculated by this formula:

$$£12 \div £2 = 6 \text{ units}$$

More useful may be to know how many articles have to be sold to achieve a profit target, and the following formula gives the answer:

$$\frac{\text{Total fixed costs} + \text{profit}}{\text{Contribution per unit}}$$

Suppose £10 profit is wanted, then 11 units have to be sold:

$$\frac{£12 + £10}{£2} = 11 \text{ units}$$

Exhibit 8–7

	Selling Price	Variable Cost	Contribution	Fixed cost	Break even Point in Units	Break even Point Calculation
	£	£	£	£		
1—— 5.00	5.00	3	2.00	12	6	£12 ÷ £2.00
2----- 5.00	5.00	3	2.00	16	8	£16 ÷ £2.00
3—— 5.50	5.50	3	2.50	16	7 (6.4)	£16 ÷ £2.50

Contribution to Sales Ratio[1]

Another variation of using the contribution for planning profit is to relate the contribution to sales revenue in terms of percentage of sales. This important percentage is called the Contribution to Sales Ratio (C/S) and is similar to the gross profit percentage used so excessively in the industry. If percentage figures are put alongside figures just used, the following results:

	£	%
Selling price	5	100
Variable cost	3	60
Contribution	2	40

The gross margin is 40%, or in other words the contribution to sales ratio is 40%. This can be used to determine BEP in value and also the turnover value to achieve a particular profit, the formulae being:

[1]Formerly known as profit volume ratio (P/V ratio).

$$\text{Fixed cost} \div \text{C/S ratio}$$

and $$\frac{\text{Fixed cost}+\text{profit}}{\text{C/S ratio}}$$

Using again the original example,

$$\text{BEP in £ turnover} = £12 \div 40\% = £30$$

$$\text{£ turnover for £10 profit} = \frac{£12+£10}{40\%} = £55$$

It can be seen that if cost behaviour is predictable then numerical tables and charts may be prepared to show the effect on profit of variations in plans, and especially in volume changes.

Multi-Activity Profit-Volume Chart

A profit-volume chart can be drawn to depict how each product, service or department contributes to profit, and for convenience they are drawn in order of profitability with the highest contribution to sales product first (C). Total fixed cost for the enterprise is marked as with a profit chart, and a line drawn showing C's contribution, then B and A.

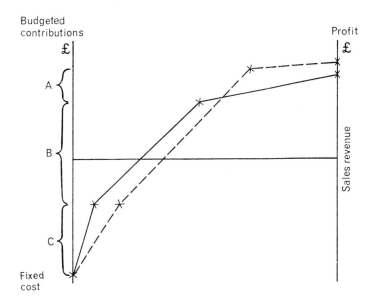

In the illustration the dotted line is actual and the other the budget. It can be seen that C's contribution was the same as budgeted but from higher sales. B's contribution to sales on the other hand improved and boosted profits but A's fell as did its sales.

A.F.M./2—H

Break-even Charts Review

Economics break-even chart
Accurate break-even charts in the form described earlier depend upon costs
and revenue being represented by straightlines (are linear). The chart is nevertheless useful if the picture provided is an approximate representation of the
data. An economics break-even chart generally shows average selling price falling as extra sales meet more competition, and the law of diminishing returns
increasing the variable unit cost.

Two break-even points result from these factors:

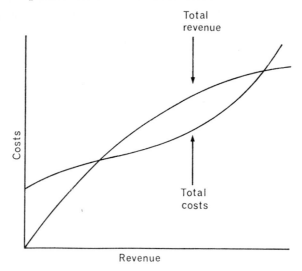

Relevant range
Although cost and revenue are shown meeting the Y axis, this is done for ease
of drawing. The chart would be true for a limited range of activity and certainly
not for low levels when fixed costs would in practice be avoided by closing
facilities.

Product mix
The revenue and variable cost lines are true of a particular sales mix only.

Finished stocks
These do not appear in the chart and therefore changes in finished stocks do
not affect the chart. There may be occasions when it would be dangerous to
make decisions using the chart but ignoring stock changes.

Cash break-even charts
Two forms of cash break-even chart are available to management, one in which
cash payments and cash receipts for a year replace costs and revenue in the
orthodox form.

The other covers any relevant period with cumulative cash being shown. It gives a profile of cash associated with an investment project and shows how many years will elapse before the investment is recovered in cash. It takes the form of a profit chart if cash inflow is constant.

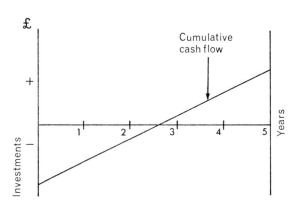

Simple Profit Planning

Operation of vending machines provides another simple profit planning example where costs again are either fixed or variable.

Let the machine be sighted outside a greengrocer's shop on a piece of ground useless for other purposes, and let it dispense drinks at 5p each. Mr. G. the greengrocer decides to load both channels with the same powder to produce drink A. Costs associated with the operation are estimated to be:

Annual hire charge and maintenance		£95
Electricity and water per annum		£5
Cost of cups £5 per 1,000	(£0·5 per 100)	
Cost of powder £1·43 per 100	(£1·5 per 100)	= £2 per 100
Estimate wastage 5%		or 2p each

Mr. G. reckons that for every drink he sells he will receive 3p (5p − 2p) and this will contribute to the £100 annual charge. To find out how many drinks he will need to sell to recover his annual charge he divides £100 by 3p to give 3,333 drinks. He estimates that 4,000 would be his first year's sales and since this is 667 in excess of his break-even point of 3,333 his profit should be 2,000p (667 × 3p). If his sales proved to be 5,000 he would expect a profit in the year of 5,000p or (5,000 − 3,333) × 3p.

A simple profit planning exercise has been described which, magnified many times, and complicated by other factors, is the sort of work hotel and restaurant managements carry out.

Progressing to the restaurant, the contribution approach can be used to assess the expected profit for different number of covers.

Suppose for some particular reason the restaurant has persuaded an extra guest to join a party of three. The value to the business of this fourth guest is simple to estimate because it is the cash received from him – say 80p – less the food cost of the dishes served – say 50p – leaving additional profit of 30p. It might be said that the extra guest contributed 30p to the profits of the business being selling price less variable cost of the sale.

If the average revenue per cover were 80p and average food cost were 50p, and annual fixed costs were £3,000, speedy calculations can be made to discover expected profit at say 10,000, 15,000 and 20,000 covers per annum. For instance profit at 20,000 covers would be £3,000 taken from 20,000 × £0·3, leaving £3,000 profit. A statement showing contribution and profit at the three levels is shown in Exhibit 8–8.

It can be seen that after the point where total contribution equals fixed cost (10,000 level), the additional contributions equal additional profit. Increasing covers from 15,000 to 20,000 brings in additional contribution and profit of £1,500 (5,000 × £0·3). If the present level of operations is 15,000 covers per annum it is clear that if £1,000 extra revenue expenditure such as advertising were to increase turnover to 20,000 covers without affecting either present contribution (gross profit) per cover or fixed costs, then £500 extra profit could be expected.

Exhibit 8–8

Profit Statement showing contribution over a range of covers

Covers (No.)	10,000	15,000	20,000
	£	£	£
Sales @ £0·8	8,000	12,000	16,000
Less variable costs @ £0·5	5,000	7,500	10,000
CONTRIBUTION @ £0·3	3,000	4,500	6,000
Less fixed cost	3,000	3,000	3,000
PROFIT	NIL	1,500	3,000

The concern here has been with the average price for the average meal which is required to achieve a total contribution and profit. However, policy often suggests that certain dishes, for instance starters and vegetables, can accept a higher than average mark up, compensating for a low gross margin on some main dishes. Several reasons could be put forward for accepting on some dishes a lower than average gross margin for the business, varying from competition restricting the price, to a deliberate policy of low prices to attract customers who would be likely to take also speciality dishes which gave above average margins.

Contribution per Unit of Limiting Factor

In circumstances where there is opportunity to change the limits of operated departments it may be advisable to enlarge the most profitable department at the expense of another department. Accordingly the floor space may be regarded as the limiting factor and a calculation made to discover which department has the highest contribution per sq. metre of floor space.

Listing departments in order of contribution per sq. metre is the start-point in a profitability study.

Forecast Profit Statement year ended . . . . .

Eg.		*Dept. A*	*Dept. B*	*Dept. C*	*Total*
1	Contribution	£2,000	£4,000	£5,000	£11,000
2	Square metres	1,000	1,000	2,000	4,000
(1 ÷ 2)	Contribution per sq. metre	£2	£4	£2·5	
	Order of profitability	3	1	2	

On the face of it, if say 500 square metres of Dept. A were to be used to expand Dept. B and B's sales increased by $\frac{1}{2}$ without dropping selling prices total contribution would be:

		Dept. A	*Dept. B*	*Dept. C*	*Total £*
1	Contribution per sq. m.	£2	£4	£2·5	
2	Square metres	500	1,500	2,000	
(1 × 2)	New total contribution	£1,000	£6,000	£5,000	12,000
	Former contribution				11,000
	Increased annual contribution				1,000

This change in contribution takes account of changes in the total cost of food and drink caused by new sales levels. If no additional fixed costs such as salaries, equipment and advertising were involved then the additional contribution of £1,000 would become the additional profit. If equipment costing £3,000 were required, depreciation of £600 per annum over 5 years would mean the increase in profit was only £400 p.a.

Other factors to be considered would be the effect on profit if any sales in Dept. A influenced sales in Dept. B. A very small contribution by one department might be the cause of a large contribution in another department, a state of affairs which might be acceptable because in the final analysis it is *total* contribution and *total* profit that counts.

A restaurant in a departmental store may show only a small contribution, but may attract customers to sales departments where good contributions are being made.

Clearly the contribution per unit of limiting factor is a useful start for a plan to increase profitability, indeed it should precede the preparation of the sales budget.

Linear Programming

If there are two different products, services or departments competing for two or more limited resources then the linear programming 'graphical technique' will provide the answer in terms of the optimal activity mix which maximizes profits. An example will illustrate the technique.

A speciality restaurant offers two groups of dishes knows as 'frieds' and 'grills', which have average contributions of £1 per dish.

	'frieds'	*'grills'*
Average labour times per dish:		
Food preparation	2 mins	3 mins
Restaurant service	5 mins	2 mins

Total food production and service available per day:
    Kitchen staff   30 hours
    Restaurant staff   40 hours
Current ingredient scarcity allows only 500 'grills' to be available per day.
Determine graphically the dish mix which maximizes contributions.

The solution is best commenced by laying out the relevant facts in mathematical form:

(a)[2] Kitchen limiting factor $\qquad$ $2f + 3g \leqslant 30$ hours
(b)   Restaurant limiting factor $\qquad$ $5f + 2g \leqslant 40$ hours
(c)   Food scarcity factor $\qquad$ $g \qquad \leqslant 500$ dishes
(d)   Maximize contributions $\qquad$ $£1f + £1g$
    As negative production is not possible f and g must be each $\geqslant$ zero.

The first three expressions may now be graphed as illustrated in Exhibit 8–9.

For example, with the kitchen limiting factor the maximum number of dishes which could be produced is:

$$\text{'frieds'} \qquad \frac{30 \text{ hrs} \times 60 \text{ mins}}{2 \text{ mins}} = 900$$

or

$$\text{'grills'} \qquad \frac{30 \text{ hrs} \times 60 \text{ mins}}{3 \text{ mins}} = 600$$

Similarly either 480 'frieds' or 1200 'grills' could be served in 40 hours. These alternatives may be plotted on the graph together with the 500 'grills' food

[2]f = 'frieds' and g = 'grills'.

Exhibit 8–9

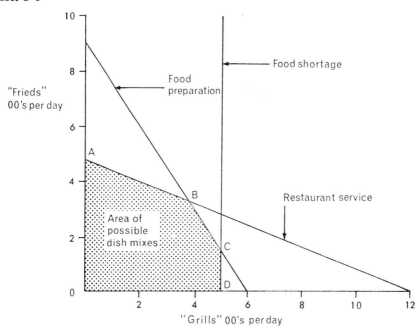

shortage. Points A, B, C, and D become the possible combinations of dishes. A ruler joining 200 'frieds' with 200 'grills' will represent all combinations of dishes to give a total contribution of £200 e.g. 200 'frieds' or 200 'grills' or 100 'frieds' and 100 'grills' etc. Keeping the slope constant and moving the ruler outwards from O, which represents increasing the total contribution, point B is the last to be reached. This point is where 327 'frieds' and 382 'grills' are produced. Maximum contribution is therefore:

					£
'frieds'	327	@	£1	=	327
'grills'	382	@	£1	=	382
					709

This is better than point C which gives:

					£
'frieds'	150	@	£1	=	150
'grills'	500	@	£1	=	500
					650

It will be noted that the food shortage is not a constraint on the optimum mix. However, if the contribution were 'frieds' .. £1 and 'grills' @ £1.60, then C would represent the best mix and the food shortage factor would become an effective constraint.

		Point B		Point C
		£		£
'frieds'	327	327	150	150
'grills'	382	611	500	800
		938		950

More complex planning problems involving more than two outputs e.g. dishes, require much tedious calculation necessitating the use of a computer.

Off-season Closing – the Financial Effect

Because of low turnover in the off-season, management might wish to consider whether closing the establishment during the off-season would improve overall profit. For this purpose it is necessary to estimate:

(a) the annual revenue and cost assuming all the year round opening, and
(b) the annual revenue and cost assuming the establishment is closed for a period.

Clearly the alternative with the highest profit would, on the face of it, be the best course of action. Different presentations may be used to show the financial comparison, but it is wise in each case to classify costs according to their behaviour, namely, variable, semi-variable and fixed.

Given the costs and revenues for a 12-month opening and an 8-month opening. Exhibit Nos 8–10 and 8–11 are examples of recommended presentations.

Exhibit 8-10

	(a) 12 months	(b) 8 months	(c) 'difference'
	£ £ £	£ £	£ £
Sales	50,000	45,000	5,000
Food & drink costs	20,000	18,000	2,000
GROSS MARGIN	30,000	27,000	3,000
Semi-variable costs			
Wages	10,000	8,000	2,000
Light, heat & power	2,000	1,600	400
Maintenance & repairs	1,500	1,300	200
Laundering	1,000	900	100
Telephone	250	200	50
Depreciation	1,500	1,000	500
Other expenses	2,750	2,700	50
	19,000	15,700	3,300
	11,000	11,300	300
Fixed costs			
Lease	1,000	1,000	
Local rates	1,000	1,000	
Other expenses	3,000	3,000	
	5,000	5,000	nil
	6,000	6,300	300
Apply 12 months opening profit		6,000	
Additional profit from 8 months opening		300	

Presentation 1 – 'Total approach'

Note: Column (c) has been introduced to facilitate the 'Differences' approach of presentation 2.

Exhibit 8-11

Presentation 2 – 'Differential approach'

Effect of closing for four months	£
Savings in annual costs (detailed)	3,300
Less: Gross margin lost	3,000
Additional profit per annum	300

It should be noted that fixed costs are not relevant to the decision.

It must be remembered that statements such as these assist in decision making, but that some factors such as goodwill are difficult to quantify and may not be brought into the financial statement. The decision in this case might be

to remain open all the year if at least £300 in goodwill, affecting future profits
to this extent, were considered.

Questions and Problems

8–1   Explain the following terms:
      (*a*) contribution
      (*b*) break-even point
      (*c*) margin of safety.

8–2   What is the 'contribution to sales ratio'?

8–3   Below is an outline break-even chart:

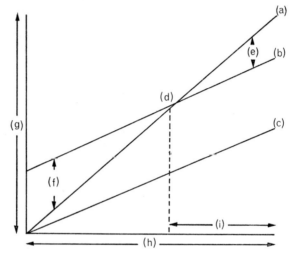

Name the various points indicated by the letters. What is the name of
the area taken in by the 'origin', (*a*) and (*c*)?

8–4   Below is the outline of a profit volume break-even chart.

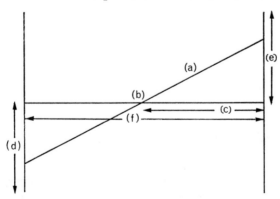

Name the various points indicated by the letters.

8–5 Accounting and economics break-even charts differ. Describe the principal differences between the charts and indicate the extent to which one is justified in using the accounting kind of chart.

8–6 Complete the following tabulation:

Annual fixed costs £	Contribution per unit £	Break-even point Units
10,000	0·50	*
*	0·85	9,000
30,000	*	20,000

8–7 The budgeted sales of three companies are as follows:

	Company 1	Company 2	Company 3
Budgeted sales in units	10,000	10,000	10,000
Budgeted selling price per unit	£2·00	£2·00	£2·00
Budgeted variable costs per unit	£1·50	£1·25	£1·00
Budgeted fixed expenses total	£3,000	£5,500	£8,000
Budgeted capacity	80%	80%	80%

From the above information you are required to compute for each company:
(a) budgeted profit;
(b) the budgeted break-even point in unit sales;
(c) the budgeted margin of safety expressed as a percentage of total capacity; and
(d) the impact of profits on a ± 10% deviation in sales.
Comment briefly on the effect of this in relation to the distribution between the company's fixed and variable expenses.

8–8 A new restaurant is to be opened for which equipment is purchased costing £12,000 and additional working capital of £5,000 is provided.
Expected annual costs are rent and rates £2,500, salaries £3,000, insurance £100, and depreciation is to be 10% per annum of the cost of the equipment. Variable costs other than food will be 30% of sales.
It will be the policy of the management to add 200% to the food cost to give selling price which will be £1·50 per cover.
From this information you are required to determine by both calculation and break-even chart:
(a) the break-even point in number of covers per annum, and
(b) the number of covers necessary per annum to make a return of 20% on capital employed.

8–9 The following information relates to three alternative forecasts A, B and C each of which has the same price and the same potential level of sales but only one can be included in the next period's budget. Present this information in a suitable graphical form and comment on it in respect of the particular problem under consideration.

	A	B	C
Selling price	£1	£1	£1
Contribution to sales ratio	20%	15%	10%
Fixed costs	£9,500	£6,000	£3,750
Estimated sales	60,000 (covers)	60,000 (covers)	60,000 (covers)

8–10 The following information is taken from the accounts of the Linda Restaurant.

	Sales £	Total costs £
Year 1	60,000	54,000
Year 2	64,000	56,400
Year 3	70,000	60,000

(a) From this information calculate the net profit to be achieved in Year 4 if sales are £80,000 as estimated and fixed costs increase by £4,000.

(b) Calculate also the break-even point when sales are £40,000.

8–11 A food processing job is done manually by employees who can each carry out 1,500 jobs in a week, and whose wages are £15 each per week. The cost of expendable supplies required in this task is £3 per 1,000 jobs.

As a result of work study investigation it is found that the task can be undertaken by a piece of equipment costing £4,000 with a capacity of up to 9,000 jobs per week. The operator would be paid £24 per week but would not be available for other work as he is a specialist operator. The present employees on this work are moved to other work should the need arise.

Costs associated with the equipment are:

Maintenance £2 per week.

Operating costs £4 per 1,000 jobs.

Expendable supplies £3 per 1,000 jobs.

The machine would be depreciated over 5 years of 50 weeks on a straightline basis with no residual value.

You are required to state the weekly level of activity in numbers of jobs beyond which there would be a cost saving to the company by having the work mechanized.

Your answer should be arrived at by each of the following methods:

1. Tabulation   2. Calculation   3. Break-even chart.

8–12 It is possible to prepare a profit/volume break-even chart from successive sets of past sales and profit figures and then to use the chart to predict future results. For any volume of sales, a figure for total costs can then be read off the chart and the fixed and variable elements of total costs isolated.

You are required to:

(a) draw a break-even chart from the following figures:

	Sales £	Profit £
Year 1	3,200,000	80,000
Year 2	3,500,000	200,000

(b) predict the variable cost, contribution, fixed cost and profit associated with £5,000,000 sales volume, and set out your predictions in the form of a profit statement; and

(c) state the main assumptions underlying predictions such as these.

8–13 Go-Ahead Hotels Ltd. offer a package holiday which during the current year has sold for £40, the variable cost being £25. The company's accountant has estimated the profit for the year at £150,000 after allowing for fixed costs of £120,000.

During discussion on the 1975 budget the hotels' controller said he anticipated a unit variable cost rise of £1 following a recent wage award. The accountant expects fixed costs to rise by £5,000 this being due, in the main, to increased rental payable under the company's leases which are currently being re-negotiated. The marketing manager thought the market was buoyant but also owing to rising costs, competitors would increase the prices of their holidays in 1975. He expressed the views that:

(i) with the price remaining at £40, the number of holidays sold next year would increase by 10%; and

(ii) if the price could be reduced by £1, increase in sales of 25% could be expected.

You are required to:

(a) present a statement to show which of the Marketing Manager's proposals provide the greater amount of profit;

(b) calculate in respect of each alternative the break-even point in terms of sales volume; and

(c) under alternative (ii) how many holidays would the company need to sell to earn a profit of £160,000?

8–14 The banqueting manager of the Sismat Hotel Group Ltd. is issued with the following procedure for calculating net profit arising from functions held in the banqueting facilities of the Group:

(i) establish food cost

(ii) charge £2 per person, to recover the Head Office fixed cost.

(iii) charge £50 per function, to recover wages of permanent banqueting staff and banqueting fixed overheads.

(iv) calculate the charge for casual labour (basis, 40p per customer, for every customer in excess of 40).

(v) wines are charged for separately. Charge based on gross profit of $66\frac{2}{3}\%$ on sales.

Three requests have been received to use the banqueting facilities, available, only one of which can be accepted.

Details of these requests are:

Request from:	Westley	Worthington	*Wilson
Number of customers	140	80	40
Total food cost	£90	£30	—
Estimated demand for wine	50 to 70 bottles	40 to 60 bottles	—
Estimated cost of wines	70p	£1	—
Price per customer (excluding wines)	£2·50	£2·20	—

*Wilson just wishes to hire the banqueting facilities for £275 and will make his own arrangements to provide the meals and drinks.

You are required to prepare:

(a) Statements showing the estimated range of net profit for each function, using the procedure laid down by head office.

(b) Statements showing the range of contribution estimated to arise from each function.

(c) A statement ranking the requests in the order in which they should be accepted, and

(d) Letter to the managing director commenting on the procedure laid down by head office for calculating net profit on banqueting facilities.   (H.C.I.M.A.)

8–15 A company which produces two food products has annual fixed costs of £12,000:

	Food product A	Food product B
	£	£
Selling price	5	4
Less: Variable costs	2	2
Contribution	3	2

The desired product mix is two of A for every one of B. You are required to show by both calculation and break-even chart how many of each food product need to be sold to break even.

8–16 Precise Limited has prepared the following budget for the forthcoming year:

	Restaurant	Canteen	Total
No. of meals	40,000	120,000	160,000
	£	£	£
Sales	80,000	360,000	440,000
Expenses:			
Food	20,000	80,000	100,000
Direct labour	4,000	140,000	144,000
Overheads	40,000	90,000	130,000
	64,000	310,000	374,000
Profit	16,000	50,000	66,000

The overhead figures contain both fixed and variable overheads. The variable element is estimated to be 30% of the direct labour expense.

You are required to:

(a) Ascertain by calculation the break-even point assuming sales remain constant; and
(b) Draw a multi-activity profit volume chart and explain why the break-even point differs from your calculations in (a) above.

8–17 The Premier Catering Company offers four menus, details of which are as follows:

	Menus			
	W	X	Y	Z
	£	£	£	£
Selling price	3	10	6	5
Less: Variable costs	1	4	4	2
Contribution	2	6	2	3

Each menu absorbs units of a limiting factor per cover i. e. Menu W, 4 units; Menu X, 10 units; Menu Y, 2 units; Menu Z, 4 units. The sales manager has carried out a market research study which has resulted in the following forecast of the maximum covers per menu for the coming period: Menu W, 20,000; Menu X, 8,000; Menu Y, 15,000; Menu Z, 12,000. Further, the total amount of limiting factor extimated to be available during the next period is 108,000 units. You are required to calculate the optimum sales mix and the total contribution which results.

8–18   A large hotel has 500 rooms divided into 200 suites and 300 double bedrooms. The hotel is full for nine months of each year but from January to March business is fairly quiet. Room tariffs, costs etc., are as follows:

	Suite	Double room
Selling price	£20	£12
Variable costs (including room servicing)	£9	£5
Room servicing times	1 hour	½ hour

Experience has shown that during the three-month period the maximum number of room lets that can be made are 4,000 suite room nights and 9,000 double room nights. The total number of room servicing hours available is estimated to be 7,000 hours.

Using the linear programming graphical technique determine the combination of suite/room lets which will yield the greatest profit.

8–19   Your company is considering the purchase of an hotel in Torquay. On the basis of past years' trading results, the estimated figures for future years' trading results are as follows:

	1st April to 30th September £	1st October to 31st March £
Sales	43,000	15,000
Other income	4,000	700
Cost of sales	23,000	8,000
Wages	14,000	4,000
Heat and light	600	700
Repairs and maintenance	500	250
Rates	1,000	1,000
Other expenses	400	50
Depreciation:		
Premises	2,000	2,000
Fittings	900	900
China, cutlery etc.	300	100

If the hotel closed during the off season, then the depreciation on fittings would be reduced to £500 and China, Cutlery, etc., £Nil.

You are required to:

(a) prepare financial statement(s) to illustrate the advisability of remaining open (or closing) during the off season periods; and

(b) if it is the company's policy to achieve a return on investment of 12%, what is the maximum price it could offer for the hotel?

8–20 A catering company has three quick-service restaurants. The profit and loss statement for 1976 was as follows:

	Quick Eats £	Quick Eats £	Swift-Bite £	Swift-Bite £	Speedy Snacks £	Speedy Snacks £	Total £	Total £
Sales		16,000		36,000		20,000		72,000
Less: Costs								
Food	5,000		6,000		4,000		15,000	
Variable overheads	7,000		12,000		6,000		25,000	
Fixed overheads	6,000		6,000		4,000		16,000	
		18,000		24,000		14,000		56,000
Net profit (loss)		(2,000)		12,000		6,000		16,000

The Quick Eats Restaurant has consistently been making losses over the last two years and the company are considering closing it down.
You are required to:

(a) show the profit and loss statement that would arise if the company did close down the restaurant; and

(b) suggest how the company could improve its profit position.

Further Reading

1. Baggott, J., *Cost and Management Accounting*, W. H. Allen; chapter 19.
2. Horngren, C. T., *Cost Accounting, A managerial emphasis*, Prentice-Hall; chapters 3 and 27.
3. Sizer, J., *An Insight into Management Accounting*, Penguin Books; chapter 8.

CHAPTER NINE

PRICING ASPECTS

ONE decision management cannot avoid is deciding the price charged for goods or services. It is only when the sale is effected that a profit (or loss) is made. Pricing to achieve a given total target profit is influenced by a large number of market factors which are outside the scope of this work. The aim here is to consider the influence that cost may have on price rather than the highly specialized study of the influence of the market place on price.

One classification of pricing methods that will help to isolate problems where a knowledge of cost can clearly be of assistance is by time scale. Two categories are long-term pricing or primary pricing, and short-term or secondary pricing.

Long-term pricing is associated with maintaining a stable price for most of the firm's turnover and for the industry as a whole. A large number of firms would add a mark-up to cost that was considered reasonable. This price would be set in the first place by market leaders to ensure their own profit was reasonable. Smaller concerns would price using the market leaders' price as a guide. Individual costs of products and services may bear little relationship to long-term prices, for company policy may vary significantly from company to company. The only example to be shown where costs are associated with long-term pricing is the first one which emphasizes the use of contribution.

Short-term pricing refers to prices which may be negotiated, such as prices of functions, and where the firm is pricing a service or product which does not conform to normal pattern of sales. In these cases it is important to know the marginal or the opportunity cost involved.

Pricing Food and Beverages

Management will have in mind a profit figure to aim for when considering the next twelve months' operations whether or not a budgeting system is installed. If this forecast profit is added to forecast fixed costs for the whole business then forecast contribution results. E.g.:

	£
Profit	2,000
Fixed costs	10,000
Contribution (gross profit)	12,000

The work of the restaurateur is to determine selling prices and food and drink costs which will produce this contribution, and a number of ways may be available depending upon policy such as a quick customer turnover of low priced meals or a more exclusive service of higher priced meals. Assuming for simplicity an average meal – Alternative A:

	£	£	%
Sales revenue 60,000 meals @	0·80	48,000	100
Less Food cost 60,000 meals @	0·60	36,000	75
CONTRIBUTION 60,000 meals @	0·20	12,000	25
Less Other costs (fixed)		10,000	
PROFIT		2,000	

How was the food cost and price arrived at? The first step might have been to determine the selling price per meal that would attract customers – a matter of policy – and to forecast the number of meals expected at that price, in this instance 60,000 meals at £0·80. The missing factor, a matter initially of calculation, is the food cost which should be £36,000 or £0·60 per meal. To price individual dishes and meals, the average percentage to add to food cost to cover contribution (fixed cost and profit) is:

$$\frac{£0\cdot20}{£0\cdot60} \times 100 = 33\cdot3\%$$

or $$\frac{25\%}{75\%} \times 100 = 33\cdot3\%$$

A meal costing £0·50 would be priced at £0·50 + 33·3% = £0·67. The relationship of this percentage, or mark up as it is called, to gross profit percentage is explained on page 135.

Alternative B might be to achieve a higher utilization of the establishment by selling 80,000 meals at an average charge of £0·40. How much must food cost per average meal be restricted to if annual fixed costs are still to be £10,000 and profit £2,000? Total contribution is still £12,000 so that known figures are:

	£	£	%
Sales revenue 80,000 meals @	0·40	32,000	100
Less Food costs 80,000 meals @			
CONTRIBUTION	0·15	12,000	37·5

Food cost must be £0·25 per meal which is 62·5% of selling price.
Pricing an individual meal will require an addition of 60% to food cost:

$$\frac{37·5\%}{62·5\%} \times 100 = 60\%$$

The important point to remember when making pricing decisions is that if costs other than the truly variable costs of food and drink are not going to change under alternative pricing plans, the immediate target becomes not a total profit but a total contribution. With fixed costs of £10,000 per annum and a profit target of £2,000, alternative policies might be quantified as follows:

1	2	3	4	5	6
% capacity	No. meals (forecast)	Required total contribution (given)	Required contribution per meal (3÷2)	Selling price (forecast)	cost per meal (5−4)
		£	£	£	£
50	40,000	12,000	0·30	0·80	0·50
67	50,000	12,000	0·24	0·70	0·46
75	60,000	12,000	0·20	0·60	0·40
82	70,000	12,000	0·17	0·50	0·33
100	80,000	12,000	0·15	0·40	0·25

Should fixed costs be expected to rise above £10,000 for any level then this must be added to the £12,000 contribution. Although 100% capacity is not normally practical, suppose an additional cost of £2,000 per annum achieved this and meal price was £0·40, then the new contribution would be £14,000 ÷ 80,000 = £0·175 per meal leaving a cost of £0·225.

Industrial Canteen Pricing

The object is often for canteen costs to be passed on to employees using the canteen so that the canteen 'breaks even'. Sometimes the company is willing to subsidize the canteen service. To price canteen dishes under a break-even policy the estimated annual costs are shown in two categories e.g.

	£	%
Food costs	10,000	100
Other costs	6,000	60
	16,000	

As no profit is involved pricing is a matter of adding a percentage to food cost which represents the percentage of other costs to food cost, in this case 60%. A dish with a food cost of £0·15 would sell for £0·24.

Where a subsidy is granted it is simply taken away from other costs. E.g.

	£	£	%
Food costs		10,000	100
Other costs	6,000		
Subsidy	2,000		
	————	4,000	40
		14,000	

With a food cost of £0·15 the dish would be priced at £0·21 (£0·15+40%).

Pricing Individual Functions

Pricing of individual jobs such as banquets needs to take into account:
  (a) Food, drink and tobacco costs,
  (b) Direct departmental costs such as casual wages,
  (c) General overheads such as local rates,
  (d) Profit.
Without doubt the price of a function must exceed the sum of (a) and (b), but how much of the price should cover (c) and (d) is a matter of policy. An exercise may be carried out annually to apportion all budgeted general overheads to operated departments in order to arrive at a budgeted total cost of these departments. If general overheads apportioned to say banqueting were related to budgeted food and drink of the department, the resulting percentage could be used to 'recover' these overheads on particular functions.

E.g.   *Banqueting Budget year ended . . . . .*

	£	£
Food cost	20,000	
Drink and tobacco cost	8,000	
	————	28,000
Direct departmental expenses		4,000
Apportioned overheads		8,000
		40,000

A target profit to turnover of 20% would require sales of £50,000, leaving a profit of £10,000. To price individual functions a mark-up of 56·25% on food, drink and other direct costs would achieve this result, calculated as follows:

$$\frac{(\text{Revenue} - \text{All direct costs})}{\text{All direct costs}} \times 100$$

$$= \frac{(\text{£}50,000 - \text{£}32,000)}{\text{£}32,000} \times 100 = \frac{\text{£}18,000}{\text{£}32,000} \times 100$$

$$= 56 \cdot 25\%$$

Therefore if the budgeted amount of banqueting business was done in the year and 56·25% added on average to direct costs to give selling price the result would be:

		£
Food, drink and other direct costs		32,000
Add 56·25%		18,000
REVENUE		50,000
	£	
Less Direct costs	32,000	
Overheads	8,000	
		40,000
PROFIT (20% on turnover)		10,000

If there was spare capacity in the budget and sales actually went up by 10% without having to reduce the predetermined mark up percentage, the extra profit above that budgeted would be 10% of £18,000 or £1,800. This also assumes that apportioned overheads, mainly fixed in nature for the business as a whole, remained unchanged. The increase in revenue of £5,000 would have been offset by an extra 10% of direct costs, viz. £3,200 leaving an extra £1,800 profit.

If business tended to fall off, a flexible pricing policy might pay off, for instance, where higher selling prices were known to be acceptable without jeopardizing repeat orders, price increases might be implemented. To attract new customers on dates when no business was booked, rather than have facilities unused, the mark up percentage might be reduced. But by how much? Theoretically a selling price equivalent to the direct cost would be the minimum when the business would make neither a profit nor a loss from the function, for costs incurred in connection with the function would be passed onto the customer. However, in practice certain overhead costs such as heating and lighting might rise very slightly and should be covered in the price. This practice of pricing in relation to one off jobs where the additional cost is regarded as the rock bottom price and anything above it is a contribution towards overheads and then profit is known as marginal pricing.

Sales Mix

As seen earlier, sales volume alone can affect pricing decisions but what of the elements that make up the volume, viz. the sales mix?

Generally customers are only prepared to pay up to a certain amount for any given item, the 'going rate', therefore, a constant mark-up on food or drink is usually impractical. Inevitably, this results in a variety of profit margin on menus, wine lists and tariffs. Take for example, the pricing of items on an à la carte menu. A reasonable approach is to achieve higher profit margins on the early courses e.g. hors d'œuvres, soups, entrées and main courses, rather than sweets, savouries or cheese. Higher margins on earlier courses takes into account the customers' diminishing marginal utility. This usually occurs after one, two or perhaps even three courses have been consumed and the diners become more satisfied and progressively disinclined to order more food. As a result of this customers have to be encouraged by cheaper prices which in turn generate lower individual profit margins.

Management, however, will require an overall percentage return on investment[1] and therefore, the proportions of the sales mix elements will need to be such as to provide an acceptable overall profit for each department, or perhaps more importantly for the business as a whole. This is a 'swings and roundabouts' kind of exercise which requires practical knowledge of each individual concern in which pricing policy is to be implemented.

Below is an example which illustrates a possible menu pricing policy:

	Sales value £	Gross profit £	Gross profit %	Mark-up %
Hors d'œuvres	4,000	3,000	75	300
Entrée	1,200	800	66·7	200
Main course	16,000	12,000	75	300
Sweet	6,000	2,000	33·3	50
Coffee	1,600	600	37·5	60
	28,800	18,400		

The overall gross profit percentage attained is just under 64%

i.e. $\dfrac{GP}{Sales} \times 100 = £\dfrac{18,400}{28,800} = 63\cdot9\%$ which would probably be regarded as acceptable.

Mark-up and Gross Profit

The percentage added to food or drink cost for determining selling price is known sometimes as mark-up. The figure added is gross profit and becomes gross profit percentage when it is related to the selling price. The mark-up and gross profit are the same figure in absolute terms, but are different percentages because the figure is related to different bases, viz. mark-up percentage relates to cost and gross profit percentage relates to selling price.

If food costs 50p and the customer is charged 75p then there has been a mark-up of 25p. If 25p is expressed as a percentage of cost (50p) the result is a 50% mark-up. However, if the mark-up of 25p is expressed as a percentage of selling price there results a gross profit percentage of $33\frac{1}{3}\%$. To establish the mark-up when the cost and gross profit percentage are known:

[1] In non-commercial catering organizations where break-even or subsidies operate management still have to maintain a pricing policy which takes into account their particular level of total costs.

Gross profit
% required   =   Mark-up of

$$50\% \quad = \quad \frac{50}{(100-50)} \times 100 \quad = 100\%$$

$$33\tfrac{1}{3}\% \quad = \quad \frac{33\tfrac{1}{3}}{(100-33\tfrac{1}{3})} \times 100 \quad = 50\%$$

$$25\% \quad = \quad \frac{25}{(100-25)} \times 100 \quad = 33\tfrac{1}{3}\%$$

Opportunity Cost

Opportunity cost may be defined as 'the value of a benefit sacrificed in favour of an alternative course of action'. It is an important concept in managerial decision making and often replaces book value when the future use of assets are being considered. Consider the following example:

Golden Hotels Ltd. were approached to cater for a Lord Mayor's banquet. Because of the prestige attached to the occasion the company was prepared to charge merely the cost, if necessary, in order to obtain the function. Amongst the requirements for the evening were 20 bottles of a wine. At that time the hotel had in stock two dozen bottles which although in perfect condition they had been unable to sell. The book value for the two dozen bottles stood at £120 (£5 per bottle). It had previously been estimated that the wine could be sold outside the business for £3 per bottle, consequently this figure was included in the cost estimate of the function. The figure of £3 per bottle may be regarded as the 'opportunity cost' as it is the value of the alternative use available at the time; namely being sold outside the business.

An example in connection with fixed assets might be where the hotel owns a garage on a site and is considering replacing it with hotel accommodation. In assessing the profitability of an extension an opportunity cost figure would be added to the accommodation cost being the net revenue forgone in giving up the garage.

Questions and Problems

9–1   Describe the following terms: total cost pricing; marginal cost pricing; gross margin pricing and going rate pricing.

9–2   Is the 'rate of return' method of pricing a variation of 'total cost pricing'? Why?

9–3   Do you consider total cost pricing to be less risky than marginal cost pricing? Why?

9–4   In the opening paragraph of his book, *Pricing for Higher Profit*, Spencer Tucker states: 'Pricing is a contest between the individual seller and the individual buyer. The market is the referee; the competitors are the jeering section. But unlike sports contests, there are few ground rules.' Expand this quotation by explaining, as if to a layman, what you think the author means.

9-5 Explain the importance of the sales volume and sales mix in determining a pricing policy. Use examples from hotel, catering or institutional activities.

9-6 Give an account of the factors you would consider before deciding upon the individual prices for:
     (a) an à la carte menu
     (b) a bar tariff

9-7 What reasons can you advance for and against having a pricing policy in a restaurant based on a fixed percentage mark-up on the food cost of each dish? Explain briefly two other methods of establishing the menu price of a dish.   (H.C.I.M.A.)

9-8 How would you approach a total pricing policy for either an hotel or a university hall of residence?

9-9 The Royal Highway Hotel Ltd., which consists of 100 double bedrooms, is planning to introduce a 'Break-a-Way Weekend' special offer during the first quarter of the new year.
     The offer provides inclusive terms (with the exception of afternoon tea) from a Friday dinner time until Sunday after luncheon with a standard of facilities comparable to normal paying guests.
     Details regarding the daily costs incurred by the hotel in respect of inclusive terms are as follows:

     Direct material, i.e. food:

	per cover £
Breakfast	0·60
Luncheon	1·00
Afternoon tea	0·40
Dinner	1·40

     Direct labour:

	per day £	
Food	7·20	serving 30 covers
Accommodation	6·40	servicing 16 rooms

     Direct expenses, i.e. laundry, etc.: £0·60 per day.
     Fixed overheads: £2 per guest per day (£4,900 per qtr.).
     The current inclusive terms are an average rate of £12 per person per day.

     Additional advertising for the weekend offer has been agreed at £1,000.

The hotel usually only achieves a low room occupancy during the quarter, but the resident director and his manager are quietly confident that the offer will attract a further 600 guests over the quarter.

Annual fixed overheads of £19,600 are applicable to an average room occupancy level of well over 80%

The price charged to the special offer customers is in no way expected to influence the normal clientele pricing policy.

You are required to:

(a) recommend a pricing policy for the 'Break-a-Way Weekend' offer which will return 5% profit on sales;

(b) prepare a statement, based on (a) above, indicating the effect on the hotel's profit for the quarter if the offer comes up to expectations and

(c) explain to the director why the principles you have applied in arriving at your results, in (a) and (b) above, may not be applicable to the pricing principles of the normal hotel business.

Further Reading
1. Moore, C. L., and Jaedicke, R. K., *Managerial Accounting*, South West Publishing Co.; chapter 17.
2. Savage, C. I., and Small, J. R., *Introduction to Managerial Economics*, Hutchinson & Co.; chapter 6.
3. Sizer, J., *An Insight Into Management Accounting*, Penguin Books; chapter 9.
4. Tucker, S. A., *Pricing for Higher Profits*, McGraw-Hill.

CHAPTER TEN

STANDARD SYSTEMS OF ACCOUNTING

STANDARD classification systems of accounts have operated in some industries for many years and a most important project undertaken in 1965–6 by the University of Strathclyde's Scottish Hotel School set out, after much research, a standard classification of accounts for the British hotel industry, forming the basis of the development of a system of standard hotel accounts. Responsibility for this development was accepted by the Hotel and Catering Economic Development Committee (E.D.C.) and after further work a standard system of hotel accounting was prepared for publication in 1969 and promoted by the National Economic Development Office following the view of the Advisory Committee on Uniform Accounts for Hotels that the system was likely to be acceptable to a majority of hoteliers. For administrative convenience the booklet is printed and published through Her Majesty's Stationery Office.

Hotel Accounting

The recommended system is designed for use by all sizes of hotel to give the hotelier a very informative appreciation of his own operation. This *raison d'être* is sufficient in itself for an hotelier to use the classification of accounts recommended. However, the further advantage is the facility it affords hoteliers of taking part in the inter-hotel and inter-motel comparison schemes organized by the Centre for Hotel and Catering Comparisons at the University of Strathclyde. Although uniform accounting and inter-hotel comparison are independent the one internal looking, the other outward looking, they have been so designed to improve the two-way communication of data between the hotel and the Centre.

The main aim of this system is to assist hotels towards more profitable operation. This is done in two ways. First, the system applies the principles of management accounting to hotels, and it can therefore provide hotel management with the information required to plan and control hotel operations and improve their understanding of their own business. Secondly the system provides a standard of classification of accounts and so can facilitate the collection and presentation to management of control information in a form which for all practical purposes is common throughout the hotel industry. Reporting to management is in the form of monthly reports comprising: a summary operating statement showing profit at various levels of control, compared with budget; a summary balance sheet; and control ratios.

Collecting Information

To understand the recommended classification and coding of revenue items it is useful to consider the two-dimensional aspect of expenses. A primary expense is defined as one which cannot be divided into two or more types of expenditure so that a primary expense account can hold only one type of expenditure.

A cost centre has been defined as the smallest accounting unit for which costs will be collected, for example a physical location, an activity or merely a convenient resting place for certain primary expenses not falling naturally into any other cost centre.

An accounting statement is in subjective form when expenditure is listed according to the total of each kind of primary expense. An example is the traditional profit and loss account in which primary expenses are listed according to the 'subject' or nature of the expenditure such as salaries, wages and electricity.

On the other hand, a statement is in objective form when expenditure is grouped according to the object or function of the expenditure. An example is the statement presented to management in which expenses are grouped in cost centres in line with responsibilities for such expenses.

It can be seen that all revenue items may be arranged to fit into a matrix as follows:

Type of Expense Accounts	Department (Cost Centre) Accounts			

This basis has been used for all costs, income and departmental accounts. Decisions taken in standardizing the system were:

(a) Is the objective analysis to be determined by physical location or activity? As the activity of supplying rooms, food, etc. is common to all hotels, this method was chosen. The departments are:

Operated departments:	01	Rooms
	02	Food
	03	Liquor and tobacco
	09	Other income
Service and other departments:	11	Administration
	12	Sales, advertising and promotion
	13	Heat, light and power
	19	General Expenditure
	21	Repairs and Maintenance

22 Plant and machinery
23 Property
31 Non-operating income and
expenditure

As can be seen, the departments are in effect cost centres by definition.
(b) What happens to primary expenses which might require to be apportioned between departments? The system allows expenses to be charged directly to more than one department, for instance laundering expenses. However, as the system is tied in with responsibility for expenses, service and other departmental expenses are not apportioned over operated departments whose heads have no direct control over such expenses.

Classification of capital account items simply follows the order of items in the balance sheet.

Exhibit 10-1 shows a summary of the recommended classification and coding of accounts with four examples using the coding system. Example 1 shows a credit to 03041, a revenue account. Example 2 shows a debit to 19221 a cost account. Example 3 shows a debit to an asset account 52625, and example 4 is a credit to a liability account. In each case only one of the double entries is stated.

Exhibit 10-1

	Revenue Items		Capital Items	
		Departmental code		*Category code*
Main code	Departments	01... to 40...	Assets	50... to 69...
			Liabilities	70... to 99...
		Account code		*Account code*
Sub code	Income accounts	..001 to ..099	Detailed	
	Cost accounts	..100 to ..599	accounts	..600 to ..999
Examples				
1. Tobacco receipts	Liquor & tobacco dept.	03... ⎫		
	Tobacco sales a/c	..041 ⎬ 03041		
		⎭		
2. Carpet shampoo	General expenditure dept.	19... ⎫		
	Cleaning supplies a/c	..221 ⎬ 19221		
		⎭		
3. Purchase of furniture			Plant, etc Furniture	52... 52625
4. Purchase from sundry trade creditors			Creditors Trade creditors	71... 71811

Presenting Routine Hotel Accounting Information

Regular information is the life blood of management. The effectiveness of this information in the planning and control of operations is dependent largely on the form and timing of its presentation.

The most common forms of presentation are:

(a) Operating Statements   (b) Ratios

Operating Statements:

A Standard System of Hotel Accounting contains recommended forms of operating statement prepared monthly, consisting of a summary operation statement supported by more detailed departmental operating statements.

Exhibit 10–2 shows examples of the two forms and the relationship between them. The full statement in each case is headed:

THIS PERIOD				CODE	ACCOUNT DETAIL	YEAR TO DATE			
BUDGET		ACTUAL				ACTUAL		BUDGET	
£	%	£	%			£	%	£	%

Ratios:

A ratio is the result of dividing a number (the numerator) by another number (the denominator) and may be expressed in various forms. When both numerator and denominator are in money terms it is common to express the relationship:

(a) as a percentage when the numerator is generally smaller than the denominator

E.g. $\dfrac{\text{Cost of sales}}{\text{Net sales}} \quad \dfrac{£1,990}{£6,000} = 33 \cdot 2\%$

(b) as 'number of times' when the numerator is generally greater than the denominator

E.g. $\dfrac{\text{Annual cost of sales}}{\text{Stock}} \quad \dfrac{£36,000}{£6,000} = 6 \text{ times}$

However, other ratios, operating ratios in particular, relate money to physical units, giving a further common form of £ per room, £ per meal, £ per guest, etc.

E.g. $\dfrac{\text{Restaurant sales}}{\text{Meals served}} \quad \dfrac{£2,460}{565} = £4 \cdot 35 \text{ per meal}$

Ratios recommended in the standard system are:

Exhibit 10–2

Exhibit 10–2 showing sample hotel operating statements. £ and % columns are omitted for simplicity. Columns are as catering operating statements Exhibits 10–3 and 10–4.

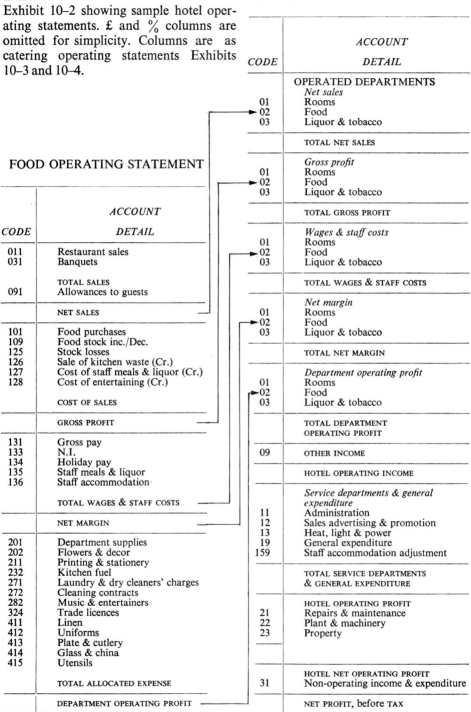

SUMMARY OPERATING STATEMENT

CODE	ACCOUNT DETAIL
	OPERATED DEPARTMENTS
	Net sales
01	Rooms
02	Food
03	Liquor & tobacco
	TOTAL NET SALES
	Gross profit
01	Rooms
02	Food
03	Liquor & tobacco
	TOTAL GROSS PROFIT
	Wages & staff costs
01	Rooms
02	Food
03	Liquor & tobacco
	TOTAL WAGES & STAFF COSTS
	Net margin
01	Rooms
02	Food
03	Liquor & tobacco
	TOTAL NET MARGIN
	Department operating profit
01	Rooms
02	Food
03	Liquor & tobacco
	TOTAL DEPARTMENT OPERATING PROFIT
09	OTHER INCOME
	HOTEL OPERATING INCOME
	Service departments & general expenditure
11	Administration
12	Sales advertising & promotion
13	Heat, light & power
19	General expenditure
159	Staff accommodation adjustment
	TOTAL SERVICE DEPARTMENTS & GENERAL EXPENDITURE
	HOTEL OPERATING PROFIT
21	Repairs & maintenance
22	Plant & machinery
23	Property
	HOTEL NET OPERATING PROFIT
31	Non-operating income & expenditure
	NET PROFIT, before TAX

FOOD OPERATING STATEMENT

CODE	ACCOUNT DETAIL
011	Restaurant sales
031	Banquets
	TOTAL SALES
091	Allowances to guests
	NET SALES
101	Food purchases
109	Food stock inc./Dec.
125	Stock losses
126	Sale of kitchen waste (Cr.)
127	Cost of staff meals & liquor (Cr.)
128	Cost of entertaining (Cr.)
	COST OF SALES
	GROSS PROFIT
131	Gross pay
133	N.I.
134	Holiday pay
135	Staff meals & liquor
136	Staff accommodation
	TOTAL WAGES & STAFF COSTS
	NET MARGIN
201	Department supplies
202	Flowers & decor
211	Printing & stationery
232	Kitchen fuel
271	Laundry & dry cleaners' charges
272	Cleaning contracts
282	Music & entertainers
324	Trade licences
411	Linen
412	Uniforms
413	Plate & cutlery
414	Glass & china
415	Utensils
	TOTAL ALLOCATED EXPENSE
	DEPARTMENT OPERATING PROFIT

A   Accounting Profitability Ratios   Form

$$\frac{\text{Operating profit}}{\text{Operating assets}}$$ %

$$\frac{\text{Gross profit}}{\text{Sales}}$$ %

$$\frac{\text{Net profit}}{\text{Sales}}$$ %

B   Accounting Liquidity Ratios

$$\frac{\text{Current assets}}{\text{Current liabilities}}$$ times

$$\frac{\text{Current assets less stock}}{\text{Current liabilities}}$$ times

$$\frac{\text{Stocks}}{\text{Daily cost of sales}}$$ days stock

$$\frac{\text{Debtors}}{\text{Daily credit sales}}$$ days credit

C   Operating Ratios (Capacity Utilization)

$$\frac{\text{Rooms occupied}}{\text{Rooms in hotel}}$$ %

$$\frac{\text{Number of guests}}{\text{Guest capacity}}$$ %

$$\frac{\text{Meals served}}{\text{Restaurant seating capacity}}$$ %

D   Operating Ratios (Average Prices)

$$\frac{\text{Room sales}}{\text{Rooms occupied}}$$ £ per room per day
(times no. days occupied)

$$\frac{\text{Room sales}}{\text{Number of guests}}$$ £ per guest per day
(times no. days stayed)

$$\frac{\text{Restaurant sales}}{\text{Meals served}}$$ £ per meal

Accounting ratios are explained in detail in the next chapter whilst operating ratios are self-explanatory.

Appendices to the Report

A   Glossary of accounting terms including the following term:

Accounts classification. An arrangement of accounting records for a definite purpose. In this report the purpose of classification is to provide accounting information for hotel management, and to provide it in a manner which is uniform to the hotel industry. A classification specifies the accounts to be used, their contents, and the sequence in which they are to be arranged.

B Basic classification of profit and loss accounts comprising:
   1. List of departments (reproduced on page 140).
   2. List of account names and their allocation to departments.
   3. An example accounts code.

C Basic classification of balance sheet accounts comprising:
   1. List of account categories (reproduced below).
   2. List of account names provided in each category together with an example accounts code.

List of account categories

Category code	Category title
50–58	FIXED ASSETS
51	Property
52	Plant and machinery
55	General equipment
56	Investments and loans
58	Goodwill
59	OTHER ASSETS
60–69	CURRENT ASSETS
61	Stocks
65	Debtors
68	Current investments
69	Bank balance and cash
70–79	CURRENT LIABILITIES
71	Creditors
79	Bank overdrafts
80–88	PROVISIONS
81	For renewal of fixed assets
82	Other provisions
89	DEFERRED LIABILITIES
90–99	CAPITAL & RESERVES
91	Share capital
92	Reserves
93	Loan capital

List of account names (e.g.)

A.F.M./2—K

Account code	Account name/or type
Property	
51601	Freehold land and buildings
51602	Depreciation of freehold buildings
51611	Leasehold – long term
51612	Amortization of long term leaseholds
51616	Leaseholds – Short term
51617	Amortization of short term leaseholds

D   Example operating statements and summary balance sheet.

    Summary operating statement and food department operating statement are shown as Exhibit 10–2.

E   Alphabetical list of accounts provided in the basic classification comprising:
    1. Account names, in alphabetical order.
    2. Allocation of accounts to departments or balance sheet categories.
    3. Example account codes.
    4. Examples of transactions allocated.

E.g. *Account*	*Allocation*	*Code*	*Examples*
Laundry and dry cleaners' charges	Rooms	01271	For linen and soft-furnishings in guest, public and cloakrooms and uniforms of rooms staff.
	Food	02271	For kitchen and table linen, and soft-furnishings in kitchens, restaurants and banquet rooms, uniforms of food staff.
	Liquor and tobacco	03271	For linen and soft-furnishings in bars, and uniforms of liquor staff.
	General expenditure	19271	For laundry and dry cleaning costs not allocated to departments.

F   Accounts dictionary comprising:
    An alphabetical list representing commodities, services, etc., commonly purchased/sold and their allocation in the basic classification.

E.g. Under the letter L

Expense item	Code	Account name	Department or group of accounts to which allocated
Laundry charges	01 02 03 19 } 271	Laundry and dry cleaners' charges	Rooms/Food/Liquor and tobacco/General expenditure

Catering Accounting

A standard system of catering accounting was published in 1971 as the catering equivalent to the hotel system, recommendations being along similar lines. This system is a natural extension wherever a catering activity is carried out within the wider sphere of an hotel operation. The basic operating functions, regarded as separate activities are:

Food preparation
Food Sales (restaurant, bar, banquet), with the addition of
Liquor sales
Liquor stockholding (cellar)

The common factor of these activities is the ability in practical terms, to identify labour with an activity and to produce a profitability statement for each. As with the hotel system other types of activity are regarded as service activities. Going beyond the hotel system, a standard costing system is now recommended to help in the control of food preparation costs. The food preparation activity is credited with the number of dishes supplied multiplied by the standard cost of each dish. This is the standard food cost for the period and the procedure enables comparison to be made with the actual food costs incurred so that the difference can be analysed into such detailed variances as are warranted. Examples of such variances were given in Chapter 7 on pages 95 and 96.

It has been considered worthwhile to reproduce three operating statements in full (Exhibits 10–3, 4 and 5) as well as extracts from them to show their inter-relationship (Exhibit 10–6).

Questions and Problems

10–1 Explain the difference between a subjective and an objective accounting statement.

10–2 What advantages are likely to accrue to an hotel owner who uses the standard classification of accounts recommended by the National Economic Development Office?

10–3 Outline the main objectives and features of the Standard System of Catering Accounting.

Exhibit 10–3

FOOD PREPARATION OPERATING STATEMENT

| THIS PERIOD | | | | ACCOUNT DETAIL | YEAR TO DATE | | | |
| BUDGET | | ACTUAL | | | ACTUAL | | BUDGET | |
£	%	£	%	CODE	£	%	£	%
				NET SALES				
9,500	74·8	9,850	74·7	Restaurant	31,220		29,700	
3,200	25·2	3,330	25·3	Banquets	10,080		9,700	
12,700	100·0	13,180	100·0	*NET FOOD SALES*	41,300	100·0	39,400	100·0
				ACTIVITY CENTRE COSTS				
3,100		3,220		101 Food purchases at standard	10,050		9,700	
120		130		109 Food stock inc./dec.	440		400	
20		20		125 Stock losses	80		70	
(40)		(60)		126 Sale of kitchen waste (Cr)	(290)		(150)	
(420)		(460)		127 Cost of staff meals (Cr)	(1,380)		(1,410)	
(400)		(360)		128 Cost of entertaining (Cr)	(1,020)		(1,140)	
2,380	18·7	2.490	18·9	*STANDARD COST OF FOOD*	7,880	19·1	7,470	19·0
2,000		2,050		131 Gross pay and other staff costs	6,420		6,200	
40		40		135 Staff meals and liquor	130		140	
150		150		136 Staff accommodation	400		420	
2,190	17·3	2,240	17·0	*TOTAL WAGES AND STAFF COSTS*	6,950	16·8	6,760	17·2
70		60		201 Supplies	180		200	
30		30		251 Kitchen fuel	90		90	
110		90		271 Laundry and dry cleaners' charges	260		300	
70		50		411 Linen and uniforms	140		150	
80		60		413 Kitchen utensils	190		220	
340	2·7	290	2·2	*TOTAL ALLOCATED EXPENSE*	860	2·1	960	2·4
4,910		5,020		*FOOD PREPARATION COSTS*	15,690		15,190	
—		100	·7	102 Materials price variance	270	·6	—	
4,910	38·7	5,120	38·8	*TOTAL FOOD PREPARATION COSTS*	15,960	38·6	15,190	38·6
				104 Food transfer charge(s) (to other activity centres)				
3,150	33·2	3,270	33·2	*022 Restaurant* } Activity	10,370	33·2	9,860	33·2
1,760	55·0	1,830	55·0	*060 Banquets* } centre codes	5,540	55·0	5,330	55·0
4,910	38·7	5,100	38·7		15,910	38·5	15,910	38·6
—		20		*FOOD PREPARATION COSTS UNDER/OVER RECOVERED*	50		—	

Extracts from food preparation operating statement

	£
Total food preparation costs	15,960
Food transfers (standard cost)	
022 Restaurant	10,370
060 Banquets	5,540
	15,910
Food preparation costs under recovered	50

Exhibit 10–6 showing

Exhibit 10–4

RESTAURANT OPERATING STATEMENT

THIS PERIOD					ACCOUNT DETAIL	YEAR TO DATE			
BUDGET		ACTUAL				ACTUAL		BUDGET	
£	%	£	%	CODE		£	%	£	%
9,600		9,980		011	Food sales	31,600		30,000	
100		130		091	Allowances to customers	380		300	
9,500	100·0	9,850	100·0		NET FOOD SALES	31,220	100·0	29,700	100·0
3,150	33·2	3,270	33·2	103	Cost of sales	10,370	33·2	9,860	33·2
6,350	66·8	6,580	66·8		FOOD GROSS PROFIT	20,850	66·8	9,840	66·8
3,140	100·0	3,250	100·0	021	Liquor and tobacco sales	10,430	100·0	10,000	100·0
1,820	57·7	1,880	57·7	113	Cost of sales	6,020	57·7	5,770	57·7
1,320	42·3	1,370	42·3		LIQUOR AND TOBACCO GROSS PROFIT	4,410	42·3	4,230	42·3
7,670	60·6	7,950	60·7		RESTAURANT GROSS PROFIT	25,260	60·6	24,070	60·6
2,500		2,440		131	Gross pay and other staff costs	7,460		7,500	
550		600		135	Staff meals and liquor	1,890		1,700	
450		410		136	Staff accommodation	1,480		1,500	
3,500	27·7	3,450	26·3		TOTAL WAGES AND STAFF COSTS	10,830	26·0	10,700	26·9
4,170	32·9	4,500	34·4		RESTAURANT NET MARGIN	14,430	34·6	13,570	33·7
130		140		201	Supplies	450		400	
80		90		271	Laundry and dry cleaners' charges	260		250	
100		130		282	Music and entertainment	340		300	
60		50		411	Linen and uniforms	210		200	
50		40		413	Cutlery, glass and utensils	110		150	
420	3·3	450	3·4		TOTAL ALLOCATED EXPENSE	1,370	3·3	1,300	3·3
3,750	29·6	4,050	31·0		RESTAURANT OPERATING PROFIT	13,060	31·3	12,270	30·4

Extracts from restaurant operating statement

	£
Cost of sales	10,370
Restaurant operating profit	13,060

Extracts from summary operating statement

Restaurant operating profit	13,060
Food preparation costs under recovered	(50)

transfers of actual year to date figures

Exhibit 10–5

SUMMARY OPERATING STATEMENT

| THIS PERIOD | | | | | ACCOUNT DETAIL | YEAR TO DATE | | | |
| BUDGET | | ACTUAL | | | | ACTUAL | | BUDGET | |
£	%	£	%	CODE		£	%	£	%
					NET SALES				
12,640	45·2	13,100	44·8	022	Restaurant(s)	41,650	46·3	39,700	46·5
6,000	21·5	6,280	21·5	032	Bar(s)	19,400	21·6	18,000	21·1
9,300	33·3	9,830	33·7	060	Banquets	28,830	32·1	27,700	32·4
27,940	100·0	29,210	100·0		*TOTAL NET SALES*	89,880	100·0	85,400	100·0
					ACTIVITY OPERATING PROFITS				
3,750	29·6	4,050	31·0	022	Restaurant(s)	13,060	31·3	12,270	30·4
1,150	19·2	1,250	19·9	032	Bar(s)	3,700	19·1	3,450	19·2
2,460	26·5	2,530	25·7	060	Banquets	7,360	25·5	7,320	26·4
7,360	26·3	7,830	26·8		*TOTAL ACTIVITIES OPERATING PROFITS*	24,120	26·8	23,040	27·0
					ACTIVITY CENTRE COSTS OVER/UNDER RECOVERED				
—		(20)		021	Food preparation	(50)		—	
—		30		031	Cellar	110			
—		—		100	Distribution	—		—	
7,360	26·3	7,840	26·8		*NET ACTIVITIES OPERATING PROFITS*	24,180	26·9	23,040	27·0
980	3·5	1,040	3·6	090	*OTHER INCOME*	2,990	3·3	2,980	3·5
8,340	29·8	8,880	30·4		*CATERING OPERATING INCOME*	27,170	30·2	26,020	30·5
					EXPENDITURE				
3,710	13·2	3,860	13·2	190	General expenses	11.460	12·8	10,960	12·9
4,630	16·6	5,020	17·2		*CATERING OPERATING PROFIT*	15,710	17·4	15.060	17·6
770	2·8	900	3·1	210	Repairs and maintenance	2,940	3·3	2,360	2·7
540	1·9	500	1·7	220	Plant and machinery	1,450	1·6	1,610	1·9
250	·9	250	·8	230	Property	760	·8	750	·9
1,560	5·6	1,650	5·6			5,150	5·7	4,720	5·5
3,070	11·0	3,370	11·6		*CATERING NET OPERATING PROFIT*	10,560	11·7	10,340	12·1
(140)	·5	(210)	·7	310	Non-operating income and expenditure	(440)	·5	(350)	·4
3,210	11·5	3,580	12·3		*NET PROFIT BEFORE TAX*	11,000	12·2	10,690	12·5

10–4　The Hotel and Catering E.D.C. has recently introduced a Standard System of Hotel Accounting which it sees as being useful, among other benefits, in the compilation of inter-hotel comparison.

　　　(*a*) List three other benefits which it is claimed will accrue if the system is widely adopted.

　　　(*b*) Distinguish between an accounts classification and an accounts dictionary in the context of a standard system of hotel accounting.

　　　(*c*) What do you understand by inter-hotel comparison?

　　　(*d*) How will uniform accounting help?　　　　　　　(H.C.I.M.A.)

10–5　The Manor Park Ltd., a medium sized hotel, has recently introduced the

'Standard System of Hotel Accounting' recommended by the Hotel and Catering E.D.C. The system has apparently worked so well as to induce the General Manager to request you to draw up the end-of-year accounts in the style of the 'Standard System'.

The trial balance for the year ended 31st March, 1976, has been extracted and agreed:

	£000's	£000's
Sales: Rooms		550
Food		250
Drink		200
Administration	70	
Sales Promotion	30	
Heat, light and power	30	
General expenses	60	
Departmental costs:		
Rooms	130	
Food	60	
Drink	60	
Repairs and maintenance	20	
Accumulated depreciation		
on equipment and fittings		
(31st March, 1975)		20
Wages and staff costs:		
Rooms	140	
Food	50	
Drink	20	
Cost of sales:		
Rooms	—	
Food	100	
Drink	100	
Loan interest	20	
Retained profit (31st March, 1975)		17
Freehold property	700	
Equipment and fittings	100	
Stock (31st March, 1976)	10	
Debtors	135	
Cash	5	
Creditors		6
Overdraft		4
Ordinary share capital		
(Authorized £1,000,000)		600
General reserve		43
Loan		130
	£1,840	£1,840

The following is relevant:

    (*a*) U.K. Corporation Tax on the year's profits is estimated at £50,000 payable before the end of the next financial period.

    (*b*) Depreciation on equipment and fittings is £10,000.

    (*c*) A dividend on Ordinary shares of 10% is proposed.

    (*d*) There are no prepaid or accrued expenses.

You are required to:

    (*a*) prepare the departmental trading, profit and loss account for year ended 31st March, 1976 (see note below); and

    (*b*) prepare the balance sheet as at that date.

Note: In answering (*a*) above you should include the following profit levels:

        (*i*) GROSS PROFIT;

       (*ii*) NET MARGIN;

     (*iii*) DEPARTMENT OPERATING PROFIT;

     (*iv*) HOTEL OPERATING PROFIT;

      (*v*) HOTEL NET OPERATING PROFIT;

     (*vi*) NET PROFIT before TAX;

    (*vii*) NET PROFIT after TAX;

   (*viii*) RETAINED PROFIT c/f.

Further Reading

1. *A Standard System of Catering Accounting*, Hotel and Catering E.D.C., H.M.S.O.
2. *A Standard System of Hotel Accounting*, Hotel and Catering E.D.C., H.M.S.O.
3. *Hotel Accounting – Introduction to a Standard System*, Hotel and Catering E.D.C.; H.M.S.O.

CHAPTER ELEVEN

MEASURING FINANCIAL PERFORMANCE

'RATIOS are the basics of the business. From the beginning we have always known what we were doing, and have always compared one place with another by the use of percentages or ratios. The system has been refined into more statistics, into graphs and so on, which are helping us to do better still.' These words are from that highly successful businessman who advocates the use of ratios, namely Sir Charles Forte.

It is usually a matter of convenience and custom that some accounting relationships are expressed as percentages and others as ratios, although all tend to come under the heading of ratios.

Two major uses of accounting ratios are:

(a) Making comparisons with other businesses to provide the basis for setting targets aimed at improving results.

(b) Making comparisons of internal results over a period of time. By this means, favourable and adverse trends are illuminated so that forecasts may be made, for instance on the basis of adverse trends being corrected.

Accounting ratios may be classified as follows:

(a) Profitability   (b) Liquidity   (c) Investment

Profitability Ratios

Return on Capital Employed (%)
Without doubt the most important ratio of any business is profit (return) related to capital employed (investment), although each of these two terms cover a number of particular meanings. The purpose of the ratio determines which measure of profit and of capital employed to use, but once selected, the choice should be used consistently.

Three of the more common interpretations are:

(a) *Measurement of management's use of total funds*
$$= \frac{\text{Profit before loan interest and tax for the year} \times 100}{\text{Capital employed (at the end of year or the average)}}$$

Capital Employed = total assets less current liabilities.

Measurement of management's use of equity funds

$$= \frac{\text{Earnings for the year} \times 100}{\text{Equity capital employed (at the end of the year, or the average)}}$$

Earnings = profit after tax, interest and preference dividend.
Equity capital = Ordinary share capital plus reserves.

(c) *Measurement of management's operating efficiency*

$$= \frac{\text{Operating profit for the year} \times 100}{\text{Operating assets (at the end of the year, or the average)}}$$

Operating profit = Profit before interest and tax, from normal operations, i.e. excluding income from investments outside the business.

Operating assets = Total assets less investment outside the business.

The performance of individual business units such as a factory or hotel is more difficult to assess because of the problem in determining the value of capital employed, which revolves around valuing the main asset, namely premises in the case of an hotel. The University of Strathclyde do not calculate this ratio in their inter-hotel comparison scheme because it has proved to be as yet impractical to prepare a fair valuation for all participating hotels which would not lead to distorted ratios. This valuation problem will eventually be overcome, but in the meantime the problem exists of valuing on a common basis, without great expense, hotels old, new, owned and leased. However, the inter-motel scheme does include this ratio as the investment in motels has been of fairly recent date, and therefore an acceptable valuation of investment has been used for comparison.

For internal planning purposes an hotel group may value each unit as it thinks fit. A comparison between hotels within a group indicates the extent to which each unit is contributing to the company return, and if one hotel's return on investment is very low, consideration would be given to improving it, using it for some other more profitable purpose, or even selling it.

Inflation is an important factor to take into account when evaluating capital employed. In the manufacturing industry, processing plant valued at cost less accumulated depreciation, gradually reduces capital employed if some profit is not retained and reinvested. Accordingly a similar profit each year on a reduced capital employed would result in an improved return, giving a false impression of improved profitability. On the other hand, freehold hotels tend to appreciate considerably in value due to inflation and other factors such as being in an area favoured by a tourist demand, and periodic revaluation of properties increases capital employed, leading to a reduced return on investment with similar annual profits. Even increased profit in a year when existing properties are revalued could well result in a considerable drop in the return on investment compared with the previous year. However, in this case, from an operating viewpoint, the position might be regarded as satisfactory. For internal purposes it is clearly important to make annual adjustments to capital employed figures to take account of inflation.

The British Institute of Management publish in their Journal *Management Today* an annual profitability league table designed to assess the profitability of the top 200 British companies. To illustrate the limitations of the return on capital employed in judging performance, some exceptional profitability changes from 1969 to 1970 give rise to the following comment in the journal, 'comparison between these two years rub in emphatically . . . that the return on investment made by a company is only one measure of management performance – and, moreover, a measure that applies only to a historical period'.

To show with what care the particular return on investment should be chosen, the table gives four different measures, the figures for J. Lyons and Co. Ltd. ranging from 4·7% to 10·7%, and an exceptional company ranging from 20·4% to 108·7%!

Profit to Sales (%)
This is the most used ratio in the industry and is not unduly influenced by valuation and inflation problems because higher costs caused by inflation are passed on through selling price increases. In businesses with unchanged capital employed this ratio would be the most important, for an increase in this ratio would mean an increase in return on capital employed, assuming a constant total sales. The relationship between profit and sales may be determined at any profit level such as departmental gross profit, departmental net margin (after wages and staff costs), departmental operating profit, and hotel gross and net operating profit as shown in Exhibit 4–2.

Sales to Capital Employed (times)
This ratio is a measure of asset utilization; the number of times assets (capital employed) are turned over in the form of sales in a year.

The relationship between these three ratios is best demonstrated with figures as follows:

Forecast	Profit/sales	× Sales/capital	= Profit/capital employed
A	$\frac{£10,000}{£100,000}$ (10%)	× $\frac{£100,000}{£100,000}$ (1·0)	= 10%
B	$\frac{£12,000}{£100,000}$ (12%)	× $\frac{£100,000}{£100,000}$ (1·0)	= 12%
C	$\frac{£12,000}{£120,000}$ (10%)	× $\frac{£120,000}{£100,000}$ (1·2)	= 12%

The management might be considering next year's budget and be faced with the choice of three forecasts, each related to a different policy.

Forecast A would repeat current results.

Forecast B would result from economies in present operations, saving £2,000 in the year.

Forecast C would result from sales promotion increasing turnover. Although the extra cost would mean that the profit/sales percentage would remain unchanged, the extra turnover achieves an extra £2,000 net profit.

The three interlinking ratios give a useful picture of past or forecast results and the first of the ratios is capable of a more detailed analysis as Exhibit 12–1. Similarly sales may be related to individual assets such as stocks; in this manner sales/capital employed ratio may be further analysed.

Liquidity Ratios

Although the general level of profit of a business may be reasonable, cash may not be available to settle debts and a liquidity problem will have arisen. It is only right therefore that ratios should measure not only profitability but also cash and other current assets in relation to demands made by creditors. Profitability ratios cover business operations for a period of time. Liquidity ratios on the other hand use items from the balance sheet to measure the ability of a business at a particular point in time to finance its current trading activities out of its liquid or near liquid resources.

Current Ratio (ratio)

Sometimes called the working capital ratio, this is the most common indicator of the ability to settle short term debts. Whilst this ratio is useful for comparisons between firms, as working capital is reduced to a form (ratio) where size of firm does not hinder comparison, for periodic comparison within a business it is the absolute rather than the relative amount which is the more important figure to study and to act upon.

The current ratio is expressed:

$$\frac{\text{Current assets}}{\text{Current liabilities}}, \text{ the denominator arranged to be 1.}$$

E.g. Current assets $\dfrac{£54,000}{£42,000}$ giving a ratio of 1·3:1
      Current liabilities

As a rough guide, if the ratio is greater than 1:1 the business is solvent, whereas a ratio of less than 1:1, say 0·7:1 may indicate a danger of insolvency. There is however a possibility of drawing wrong conclusions from such secondary data as ratios if the primary data (absolute working capital) is not studied. For instance if an overdraft is regarded as a current liability the ratio may well be below 1:1 and yet the real liquid position may be satisfactory. Another acceptable reason for the position to be apparently bad would be the sure knowledge of immediate cash being received from a fixed asset sale.

A high current ratio of say 5:1 might be regarded as high in the hotel and catering industry, indicating, after studying further ratios of other firms, the stock holding to be unnecessarily high. However, another industry, say distilling, where stocks need to be held for several years to mature, may have an average current ratio of 5:1 because of high stock values which are essential to the business.

Current ratios give only a general indication of working capital relationships, with other ratios that now follow, providing the necessary detail.

Liquid or Acid Test Ratio (ratio)
This is also called the Quick or Quick Asset ratio. The ability of a business to meet its immediate obligations is measured by comparing its current assets, excluding stocks, with its current liabilities, and a ratio of at least 1:1 would be expected to show a satisfactory liquid position, for instance:

$$\frac{\text{Current assets (excluding stock)}}{\text{Current liabilities}} \quad \frac{£44,000}{£40,000} \quad \text{ratio} = 1\cdot1 : 1$$

Stocks are excluded on the grounds that the proceeds from sale of stocks will not be received for some little time. On the other hand quoted investments if not made for trade purposes, since they may be quickly sold for cash, may be included.

Again, too low a ratio may indicate insolvent conditions, and too high a ratio may mean liquid assets are too great and are being mismanaged.

For internal assessment of the very short-term position, absolute rather than the relative position is best considered, and if cash flows are forecast the ratio may be limited to items receivable and falling due within say 3 months.

Stock Ratio (days or times per annum)
This is more explicitly termed Stock Turnover Ratio. Of the several versions of this ratio, a common one for hotel and catering is in expressing cost value of stock at the year end relative to average daily costs of sales.

$$\text{E.g.} \quad \frac{\text{End of year stocks of liquor}}{\text{Average daily cost of sales}} \quad \frac{£6,000}{£100} \quad \text{Ratio} = 60 \text{ days}$$

This indicates that it takes on average 60 days to turn stock over into sales. If this appears a slow turnover rate compared with other firms, either sales might be increased without increasing stock or if extra sales cannot be achieved, stock might be capable of some reduction. In the one case more profit should be earned from additional turnover, alternatively the saving in stock holding might be used elsewhere in the business to earn profit. If 50 days' stock were considered a target, this could be achieved by increasing turnover by 20% or by reducing stock by 16·7%.

$$\frac{\text{Stock}}{\text{Daily cost of sales}} \quad \frac{£6,000}{£120} = 50 \text{ days}$$

$$\frac{\text{Stock}}{\text{Daily cost of sales}} \quad \frac{£5,000}{£100} = 50 \text{ days}$$

Another version is the ratio of cost value of stock to cost of annual sales which gives the number of times stock is turned over per annum.

E.g. $\dfrac{\text{Annual cost of sales } £36,000}{\text{Stock} \qquad £6,000} = 6 \text{ times}$ improving to:

$\dfrac{\text{Annual cost of sales } £36,000}{\text{Stock} \qquad £5,000} = 7{\cdot}2 \text{ times}$ with a stock reduction

Average stock may be used if it is considered that year end stock figure is not representative of the average stock holding. If cost of Sales is not available then Sales Value may be used.

Debtors' Ratio (days)

This is more explicitly termed Debt Turnover Ratio or Collection Period for Debts, and indicates the average length of period of time for which credit is given by the company.

For internal analysis the amount of credit sales can be segregated from cash sales and only the former used to calculate the ratio, which is similar in some ways to stock turnover ratio.

E.g. $\dfrac{\text{Average debtors} \qquad £120,000}{\text{Average daily credit sales} \quad £2,000} = 60 \text{ days}$

For external analysis where the two types of sale cannot be separated, the total sales are usually used as the distortion tends to be low although it does not imply that proportions of credit and cash sales are constant for firms being compared, and also constant over the periods studied.

Alternative ratios are in weeks and number of times per annum the debtors are turned over.

An increase in number of days over a period of time indicates longer credit is being allowed to customers and may call for better control.

Creditors' Ratio (days)

This ratio, also named Creditor Turnover Ratio, is the average creditors' relative to average daily credit purchases, and a low number of days indicates possibly that better credit terms may be negotiated. This ratio has much in common with the debtors' ratio.

Investment Ratios

Ordinary shares are very sensitive to expected future company performance. Investors expecting good trading results later in the year, will increase demand for the shares which will push the price up until the anticipated results are reflected in the price. Should the results fall short of the standard set in the price, the price will tend to fall. Changes in share price therefore reflect not only management's past performance but also expected future results, and so the market price is unable to be used as a measure of management's past performance, especially as this is required in detail. This is measured by accounting and other ratios.

However the share price is an essential ingredient of ratios which help the financial manager and the investor. These ratios are used in the study of a company's results and dividend policy relative to the market price of its shares.

Four ratios help to interpret the following information available from published company accounts:

		£
(a)	Nominal value of ordinary shares 200,000 of 50p each	100,000
(b)	Market value of ordinary shares 200,000 of 100p each	200,000
(c)	Earnings (profit after tax, interest and preference dividend) 5p per share	10,000
(d)	Declared dividend – 8% gross or 4p per share	8,000

Earnings yield (%)
This is obtained by relating earnings to the market price of ordinary shares, or earnings per share to market price per share.

It indicates the effective return to shareholders based on the most recent earnings and for a particular share price.

$$\text{E.g. } \frac{c}{b} \times 100 = \frac{5p}{100p} \times 100 = 5\%$$

Dividend yield (%)
This relates dividend per share to market price of each ordinary share.

$$\text{E.g. } \frac{d}{b} = \frac{4p}{100p} \times 100 = 4\%$$

The difference between this ratio and the earnings yield is measured by the dividend cover ratio as follows.

Dividend cover (times)
This indicates the number of times the dividend paid goes into the earnings, in other words, the earnings yield divided by the dividend yield.

$$\text{E.g. } \frac{c}{d} = \frac{5p}{4p} = 1 \cdot 25 \text{ times}$$

Price earnings ratio (ratio)
This is another way of stating the relationship between earnings and market price of an ordinary share (earnings yield). It is the reciprocal of the earnings yield in that market price per share is divided by earnings per share.

$$\text{E.g. } \frac{b}{c} = \frac{100p}{5p} = 20$$

The company is said to have a P/E ratio of 20.

Working Capital Management

The primary object of management is to achieve profit targets – once set – over a number of years. To merely ensure the firm continues in operation, an important short-term target has to be met continually without fail, and that is the ability of paying debts and other obligations as they fall due, otherwise it becomes insolvent. Herein lies the function of working capital management. A balance should be struck between having too much and too little working capital, an objective that can only be achieved with any degree of accuracy through regularly updated forecasts and budgets of each element of working capital. Too much working capital means that opportunity is being lost of using long-term investment inside or outside the business simply because the surplus is not recognized. Too little working capital endangers the very existence of the firm, so that it is clear that to err on the high side is the better course.

The major elements of working capital within the control of management are stocks, debtors, short-term investments, cash at bank and in hand, bank overdrafts and creditors. Ratios involving working capital items are useful in forecasting the working capital level, mention having been made already of current ratio, liquid ratio, stock ratio, debtors ratio, and creditors ratio. A policy decision is needed to determine target levels of ratios of each item, for instance the number of days' stock holding and the number of days' credit allowable to customers. Whilst past experience and comparison with similar firms may be the only way of assessing target cash and stock levels, debtor and creditor levels can be more clearly defined using ratios.

Overtrading

This is a shortage of liquid funds caused by expansion of sales without sufficient additional capital to back up the operation. Businesses which give credit to customers and hold large stocks are, however, more prone to overtrading than many hotel and restaurant concerns.

To expand sales usually demands a higher level of debtors and stocks, which if not completely offset by extra credit allowed from suppliers means holding more working capital investment. Where is this to be obtained? If overdraft facilities are fully stretched before expansion, difficulty is likely to arise in obtaining more cash with which to fund the difference.

A difficult situation usually arises in overtrading when through lack of cash, creditors are kept waiting for their money and they become reluctant to supply goods on credit, debtors are chased for earlier settlement and offered attractive discounts, or cash customers are offered cut price sales to turn over faster the stocks. In any case profit is likely to suffer.

Undertrading is the opposite of overtrading in that sales are too low in relation to capital resulting in low profits. However the cash position may be healthy unless too much is taken out of the business by shareholders.

Balance Sheet Limitations

Ratio analysis aids interpretation of the financial position of a business by concentrating attention on relationships of items making up the final accounts. As the balance sheet shows the financial position at one point in time, a few days' transactions could change the whole picture almost overnight, although this by no means invalidates the study of relative and absolute figures for the purpose of assessing the health of a business.

An overdraft shown and treated as a current liability could result in a liquid ratio of much less than 1:1 yet no liquidity problem may exist as the overdraft is unlikely to be withdrawn.

Valuation of land and buildings may take place only once in five years so that in the interim years they would be undervalued in a period of inflation. E.g. as in 1968 J. Lyons and Co. Ltd. revalued land and buildings adding some £25 million to the value of assets. Hotel companies owning their own hotels are constantly benefiting by inflation because these increasingly valuable assets do not in the short term need replacing. However, any plant and machinery owned needs to be replaced at some future time when inflation will have added to the cost of replacement. Unless the difference between original cost and replacement cost is set aside over the years and not distributed to shareholders, there may be a problem of finding the extra finance for the firm to stay in the same position.

In businesses where much replacement of assets is needed and all profits are distributed, then it may be said that capital is being eroded in that asset values and therefore capital employed is in real terms reducing in value.

Questions and Problems

11-1 Compare and contrast 'profitability' and 'liquidity' ratios.

11-2 The gross profit percentage is one of the most closely controlled ratios within the hotel and catering industry. Why do you think this is so?

11-3 What factors should a manager be aware of when reading a financial performance report containing various accounting and operating ratios?

11-4

Firm	Sales	Net Profit	Capital Employed	Net Profit Ratio	Net Turnover	Return on Capital Employed
	£	£	£	%	No. times	%
A	200,000	30,000	160,000	*	*	*
B	40,000	*	*	5	2	*
C	*	3,000	*	10	*	5
D	*	*	400,000	*	6	8
E	900,000	*	300,000	3	*	*

Compute the missing figures indicated by *.

11–5　The following are the end-of-year accounts of the Bridge Hotel:

Trading, Profit and Loss Account for year ended 31st December			*Balance Sheet as at 31st December*	
	£	£		£
Sales		120,000	Freehold premises	71,000
Opening stock	7,400		Kitchen plant (net)	5,450
Purchases	51,000		Fittings	7,050
	58,400		Stocks	8,000
Less: Closing			Debtors	17,700
stock	8,000	50,400	Bank balance	8,400
GROSS PROFIT		69,600	Cash balance	600
				118,200
Less:				
Wages and			Capital	68,200
staff costs	30,000		Profit	16,800
Expenses	22,800	52,800	Loan	20,000
			Creditors	11,600
NET PROFIT		16,800	Accrued expenses	1,000
			Advance bookings	600
				118,200

Other information
(a) Average daily cost of sales; food £60; liquor £80.
(b) Average daily credit sales £240 and credit purchases £150.
(c) Debtors and creditors at the beginning of the year were £13,500 and £8,400 respectively.
(d) Stocks at the beginning of the year; food £700; liquor £6,700.
(e) Stocks at the end of the year; food £1,100; liquor £6,900.

You are required to calculate the various profitability and liquidity ratios you consider to be relevant in assessing the financial performance of this hotel. Comment on your results.

11–6　The following relates to Wheelers Catering Company:

Trading, Profit and Loss Account for year ended 31st March, 1977		*Balance Sheet as at 31st March, 1977*	
	£		£
Sales (all on credit)	100,000	Fixed assets (net)	
Less: Cost of sales			
		Stock	
Less: Labour and		Debtors	
expenses		Cash	Nil
Net profit before tax			

Less: Corporation tax			£
Less: Dividend paid		Share capital	50,000
Retained profit c/f	Nil	Retained profit c/f	Nil
		Creditors	

Given the following ratios you are required to fill in the missing figures in the outline final accounts:

Turnover to capital employed	2:1
Average collection period*	18 days
Acid test ratio	1:1
Stock turnover period*	36 days
Gross profit	60%
Net profit before tax	15%
Corporation tax	50%
Ordinary share dividend	15%

*Assume a 360 day year

11–7 From the following information prepare a trading, profit and loss account and balance sheet:

Issued share capital	£36,000
Working capital	£6,000
Rate of turnover of capital employed	2
Rate of stock turnover (times)	12
Current ratio	1·6:1
Debtors' ratio	0·075:1
Acid test ratio	1·1:1
Labour and expenses in relation to sales	20%

Notes: 1. Capital employed is to be taken as issued share capital plus net profit.
2. Ignore depreciation and appropriation of profits.

Further Reading
1. Clarkson, G. P., and Elliot, B. J., *Managing Money and Finance*; Gower Press; chapter 7.
2. Wood, F., *Business Accounting* (Vol. II), Longman; chapter 47.

CHAPTER TWELVE

INTER-FIRM COMPARISONS

TO maintain financial control, internal performance targets must be set in various sections of the business and performance monitored for comparison with the targets. Targets so far considered are budgets, for instance a departmental sales budget; standards such as the quantity of food for a dish; and financial and liquidity ratios.

Although the level of these targets is for management itself to decide, assistance in setting them can come from a knowledge of the performance of similar firms, most industries having access to this information in some form of inter-firm comparison scheme. The Centre for Inter-Firm Comparison (C.I.F.C.) organizes schemes for many industries, whilst some schemes are run by trade associations or other interested bodies. Hotel and catering firms can avail themselves of the services of the Scottish Hotel School, University of Strathclyde which operates both an hotel and motel scheme.

The Inter-Hotel Comparison Scheme

This scheme is one whereby financial and operating figures are collected in strict confidence from a range of hotels, processed and used by the Strathclyde Centre to enable an hotelier to compare the performance of his hotel with others of like type. The first hotel scheme was instituted by the University of Surrey in 1967 with the aim of providing 'norms' or standards by which hoteliers could judge their own performance, such standards being in the form of a percentage, ratio, or index number. To assist hoteliers determine their own target standards, ratios of three (unidentified) participating hotels are published for each factor under consideration (e.g. profit per 1,000 sq. ft.), the particular ratios being named lower quartile, median and upper quartile. To determine which of the values from a number of hotels become these three, all values are placed in ascending order, known as an 'array', and the median value is the value of the middle item. The median is an average giving a better indication of the typical value than the more common arithmetic average which may be influenced unduly by extreme values. The median has the virtue that it must be one particular value from the whole range whereas an arithmetic average may not represent a specific hotel.

The value of the item halfway between the lowest valued item and the median is the lower quartile, and similarly the item halfway between the median and the highest valued item is the upper quartile. Half the items are therefore between the quartiles which therefore give some indication of the spread of values around the median. Percentiles are similar to quartiles but show the percentage figures instead of only the items at quarterly intervals.

Suppose the percentage profit on sales submitted by 11 hotels were:

Hotel	A	B	C	D	E	F	G	H	I	J	K
%	34·9	29·4	25·3	49·3	39·9	66·9	31·2	35·2	43·1	54·1	37·1

Placed in an array they would appear:

Hotel	C	B	G	A	H	K	E	I	D	J	F
%	25·3	29·4	31·2	34·9	35·2	37·1	39·9	43·1	49·3	54·1	66·9
Order	1	2	3	4	5	6	7	8	9	10	11

The hoteliers would be informed of the three values representing the median and the quartiles as follows:

Lower quartile (11 items +1) $\times \frac{1}{4}$ = 3rd item = 31·2% (G)
Median   (11 items +1) $\times \frac{1}{2}$ = 6th item = 37·1% (K)
Upper quartile (11 items +1) $\times \frac{3}{4}$ = 9th item = 49·3% (D)

Hotel owner K would know that he produced an average percentage because as many hotels submitted lower figures as produced higher ones. He would, know also, because of the quartiles, that the hotels with higher figures than his tended to be of relatively higher value than those below, the quarter below dropping only 5·9% (37·1–31·2) whilst the quarter above going up by 12·2%. If he aimed to reach the upper quartile and be near the top he would know he had 12·2% to go.

Hotel owner J with 54·1% would know that he produced a higher percentage than over three-quarters of the participating hotels, which may give him cause for satisfaction. However, another factor, say profit per 1,000 sq. ft., may show him to be near the bottom of the table accounting for only an average overall result.

Hotels in the scheme are classified by size, etc., so that fair comparisons may be made, but even so, variations within classes do exist and these are taken into account when interpreting data. The most profitable hotel will not have a top rating in every factor comparison, for it may have a high reputation for the supply of drinks and therefore hold large stocks as a matter of policy, putting it above the upper quartile for the number of days' supply in store. The aim generally here may be to be near the lower quartile.

Each hotelier, then, uses the published data to provide himself with a target figure for each percentage ratio and index, raising sights where he would expect to produce better relative results, and ensuring that results in other areas he regards as satisfactory are maintained.

Comparative data presented include:
(a) The Size and Composition of the Sample:
    Proportion of hotels in the scheme owned by public company, private company, partnership/sole owner.

Number of hotels operated by participating companies – single unit, 2–5 hotels, over 5 hotels.

Sales mix of the hotels by department, size, price, location, bias.

Seasonality of hotels – seasonal, non-seasonal.

Breakdown of individual floor areas in total sample.

(b) Sales and Operating Statistics:

Sales trends using 1966 as index 100.

Moving annual total of bed occupancy as a percentage of last year.

Actual room sales as a percentage of maximum attainable room sales, also known as MAR – maximum attainable revenue.

Food sales per sq. ft. of kitchen and restaurant area.

Restaurant and kitchen: sq. ft. per cover.

Accommodation sales per room and per bed.

Departmental sales per employee.

Number of employees related to number of guests.

Average number of days' supply of food and drink.

(c) Cost and Profit Statistics:

Percentage cost and profit to sales, listing nearly 30 expense items.

Departmental analysis of goods sold and wage costs.

Wage per employee.

Departmental analysis of major costs by (a) sales bias (b) price of bedrooms (c) size of sleeper places.

Inter-Motel Comparison Scheme

In 1969 the first motel survey was conducted on similar lines to the hotel survey. A significant difference was the inclusion of a profit to capital employed ratio because of the relative ease with which capital costs can be calculated, having been incurred within the last few years.

Inter-firm Comparison in Other Industries

Originally inter-firm comparison schemes were based on a uniform costing system for the industry to assist in forming a common selling price policy, but more recently the emphasis, like the inter-hotel scheme, has been to aid management effectiveness.

The largest and oldest trade association is run by the British Federation of Master Printers dating from 1915 and whose 'Ratios for Management' scheme started in 1958. The Cotton Board Productivity Centre started a scheme in 1962.

The Centre for Inter-Firm Comparison (C.I.F.C.) was set up in 1959 by the British Institute of Management in association with the British Productivity Council to compare performance of firms in the same industry. They have had much success in installing and operating schemes within industries and in 1970 some 60 industries were covered by their schemes.

Exhibit 12–1

PYRAMID OF INCOME AND EXPENDITURE RATIOS

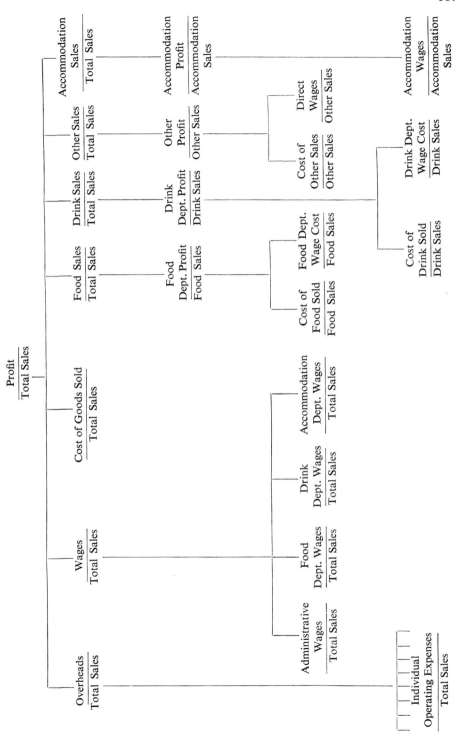

The C.I.F.C. schemes are based on the assessment of ratios, the principal ones being:

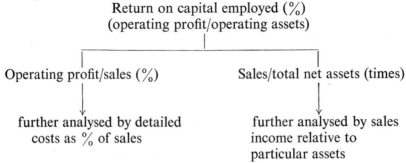

Return on capital employed (%)
(operating profit/operating assets)

Operating profit/sales (%)   Sales/total net assets (times)

further analysed by detailed   further analysed by sales
costs as % of sales   income relative to
                                             particular assets

It should be noted that these ratios were considered in the previous chapter, and that the important profit/sales is analysed under the inter-hotel comparison scheme, as in Exhibit 12–1.

Questions and Problems

12–1   Explain what is meant by quartiles when dealing with a large number of recorded items such as the number of days' stock of food relating to 100 similar type hotels.

12–2   From the following recorded data state the median, lower and upper quartiles as well as the 10, 60 and 90 percentiles.

22, 30, 16, 14, 25
16, 40, 45, 30, 38
27, 28, 13, 19, 22
41, 31, 33, 39, 29
27, 24, 41, 21, 20
12, 18, 33, 29, 16
28, 21, 33, 40, 42
41, 19, 22, 15, 39
41, 28, 16, 19, 26
25, 18, 17, 22, 23

12–3   Discuss the benefits likely to accrue to the participator of an Inter-Firm Comparison Scheme.

Further Reading

1. *Reports on the Inter-Hotel and the Inter-Motel Comparison Surveys,* University of Strathclyde.

CHAPTER THIRTEEN

THE RIGHT SOURCE OF FINANCE

EARLY in the life of any business cash is needed to pay for the use of premises and equipment, for the services of personnel and for raw materials such as food in a catering establishment. Assuming good demand exists for the product and the business satisfies that demand, it is the manner in which finances are managed that separates the successful from the unsuccessful business. The successful business man borrows money on a short-term basis and so times his operations as to collect cash from sales in time to settle bills for food, wages, etc. A very profitable product will leave him with sufficient cash to repay fairly quickly his loans and to retain cash in the business so as to increase his resources such as premises and stocks and enabling him to earn more profit. That is the way fortunes have been made. Cash for expansion is provided by the business itself. However, in hotel and catering the very profitable product with the fantastic demand rarely exists, yet the manner in which the finances are managed does provide an example of the importance of 'internal funds'.

The Sole Trader

The decision to expand
If the small business prospers its owner will be faced with the difficult decision to use his profit either to improve his own standard of living or to reinvest it in the business, and it is very largely upon which way this decision goes that the subsequent history of his business will depend.

Reinvestment of profits goes by other terms such as reinvestment of cash or earnings, ploughing back profits, retaining profit or funds, and internal funds; it is essentially a matter of the owner sacrificing cash for personal spending in order to improve the strength and earning power of his business still further.

Seldom does profit generated in a period coincide with extra cash being available at the end of the period, for after the first year's trading food consumed but obtained on credit would mean a higher cash inflow than profit made; on the other hand purchase of any resource paid for but carried forward to the next period such as stocks of food and book value of equipment would result in a smaller increase in cash in the period than profit achieved. This important consideration is explained further in Chapter 14.

If the firm continues to prosper a decision has to be made between turning away customers or providing facilities to cater for their needs. We are concerned with the hotelier/caterer who feels he wants to take advantage of the favourable position of his establishment; not with the man who is content to carry on earning a reasonable living and let chances of an improved standard of living pass him by. To many people and especially more dynamic business men, the attitude of the latter – the anti-expansionist – may seem extraordinarily short-sighted. In the end, however, business goals are an intensely personal matter. There is no law against running a business simply to earn a comfortable living, however deplorable this attitude may be to those who think all businessmen should be go-getting tycoons. Problems of finance and loss of control and contact with customers are a real dis-incentive to expand to many people owning small establishments, so that it is not surprising that they sell out at a good profit to the large company instead of developing the firm themselves.

Retained Profits

Should he decide to expand the business, the owner will consider what cash is available from 'ploughed back' profits, shown in the balance sheet as reserves or capital (liabilities) and as surplus cash or short-term investments (assets), for this is the best and cheapest source of finance for expansion. Otherwise external long term finance must be obtained, or such other sources such as leasing. There is a great temptation to use short-term funds for expansion, such as better credit facilities from suppliers, reduction in stocks and debtors and increased overdraft facilities at the bank. It is right to do these things to make better use of resources, but if the proceeds are used to invest in long term assets such as property and equipment for increasing turnover, there is a grave danger that financial difficulties will arise because with extra funds sunk in long-term assets and the planned additional turnover achieved, more short-term funds will be needed to provide additional stocks. Careful cash planning by using cash forecasts is helpful in this situation. Control of working capital is considered in Chapter 11.

Loans and Overdrafts

The clearing banks can properly claim to be the principal source of external finance available to small firms. Particularly is this the case in the formative and early development stages when much is likely to depend on the support of the branch bank manager who is prepared to back his judgement of the business acumen and vitality of the personalities involved. Bank lending is traditionally recognized to be the provision of short-term assistance for working capital purposes. The bank overdraft is the cheapest and most convenient form of short-term finance. A customer granted an overdraft is permitted to draw cheques up to an agreed figure beyond the amount standing to the credit of his account. The period of the arrangement varies according to individual require-ment; the maximum term is usually 12 months, after which the arrangement is reviewed. Interest is assessed only upon the daily cleared debit balance, and rates of interest, tied to bank rate, are significantly lower than rates charged by any other type of lender. This is especially true of the small firm paying a rate which is seldom more than 2% above that charged to the highest class of commercial undertaking, and normally in the region of 1 to 2% above bank rate. The borrower may therefore find the cost rising in times of government restriction, whereas the interest on a loan which has been negotiated for a given term remains fixed in accordance with the terms of the loan. A further disadvantage is that the overdraft may not be renewed.

A loan account with the bank is an alternative facility to an overdraft, by means of which the total amount is advanced by way of lump sum which is credited to the customer's current account balance, to be drawn upon as and when required. Loans may be granted over periods similar to those applicable to overdrafts and subject to periodic review. In agreeing to provide a loan the bank manager will satisfy himself that the money is likely to return sufficient cash to the business to allow repayments to be met. The loan must be self-liquidating, in the sense that the loan is quickly repaid.

Finance available to the small business may be obtained when property is used as security for a loan. Property may be mortgaged to obtain ready cash or may be sold to a property company who would agree to lease the premises back.

Partnerships and Companies

Transition to a Company
Entering into a partnership agreement is a further way of obtaining more funds whereby an agreed sum will be contributed to the business as initial capital. A partnership is in a position to borrow from investment institutions on mortgage and in other ways although it is often difficult to raise substantial amounts of capital without offering a share of the business. A partner investing without taking part in management may limit his liability to the extent of his subscription and this constitutes a limited partnership. The cost of raising funds is relatively low, for others may be persuaded to join the partnership at a nominal charge.

The disadvantages to the sole trader of taking a partner in a business are:
1. He loses control of the management of the business.
2. He must share profits.
3. He is subject to the risk that his partner may involve the firm in exceptional unbearable liabilities.
4. He, as founder partner, puts his private assets at stake.
5. Disposition of his share in the business is restricted.

As a partnership business grows and more cash is required consideration would be given to increasing the number of partners and possibly the formation of a limited company.

One factor limiting the size of a business is the number of members and this is summarized as follows:

| | Number of Members | |
	Minimum	Maximum
Partnerships	2	20
Private limited company	2	50
Public limited company	7	no maximum

When a choice exists, for instance when there are or will be ten members in the business, professional advice of an accountant would be sought and full consideration given to such matters as formation costs, taxation, rights and restrictions of members.

The conversion of a partnership into a private limited company involves ending the partnership which is sold as a going concern to the new company, the partners becoming shareholders and most likely directors.

However, unless expressly forbidden by the memorandum or articles of association, a private limited company may become a public limited company by passing a special resolution, filing the prescribed statement in lieu of prospectus and prescribed statutory declaration with the registrar of companies.

The public company's shares are fully transferable from one person to another and may be quoted on the Stock Exchange although this is not statutory. Of over 400,000 registered public and private companies in 1965, only about 4,600 had Stock Exchange quotations, but profits of these companies were estimated to amount to more than all the other companies put together.

Any further reference made to a company will assume it to be a public limited company with quoted shares, unless otherwise stated.

Ordinary Shares (called Equity Capital)

Holders of ordinary shares accept the main risk involved in investing in a limited company but on the other hand stand to gain most when the company makes a high profit. To all intents and purposes ordinary shares are irredeemable and are treated as a permanent investment in the firm. Under conditions of inflation ordinary shareholders tend to keep in step with inflation and more particularly where hotel and restaurant premises are owned because of the significant rise in land and property values.

After all expenses, preference share dividend and taxation payments have been met, any surplus revenue benefits ordinary shareholders in the form of dividend distribution and share value appreciation following the ploughing back into the business of any residual surplus.

At the annual general meeting the board of directors declare a percentage dividend on the nominal value of shares after a consideration of the financial position. In many cases an interim dividend will have been paid in the middle of the financial year, a payment 'on account'.

The ordinary shareholders are entitled to share pro rata in the assets distributed after a forced or voluntary liquidation.

Rights Issue

A company making a definite offer to its own shareholders to take up new shares is said to make a rights issue. The price is usually below market price as an attraction. Although an apparently attractive price may be asked of shareholders, they may benefit more from an alternative source of capital such as a debenture issue. Holders of shares to whom the offer is made may take up their rights or may sell them.

Bonus Issue

Where a company's reserves are considerable and the market price of ordinary shares far above the nominal value, a bonus issue of new shares may be made to shareholders without a charge to them. The issue is in proportion to existing shares held such as an issue of one new share for every one held.

The total market share value, and similarly each shareholder's value of his holdings, will initially remain unchanged although the market price per share will tend to drop proportionately.

A lower declared dividend percentage will provide the shareholder with the same total dividend as before, which may be an advantage from a public relations viewpoint.

A scrip issue is another term for a bonus issue.

Deferred Ordinary Shares

These rank for dividend after other ordinary shares, and usually entitle the holder to the profits then remaining. When profits are high the deferred shareholders take a substantial proportion of them.

Sometimes called founders' shares, they may be issued to managers as a form of incentive to high performance.

They are normally few in number and therefore of no great consequence.

Preference Shares

Although part of the company's share capital, these shares generally attract limited voting rights or no voting rights at all, and since dividends are at a fixed rate, preference shares have much in common with debentures.

These shares, however, are a relatively expensive source of capital compared with debentures because dividends are paid from after tax earnings, whereas debenture interest is an expense which reduces taxable profit. With corporation tax at 45% it costs the company the same to pay interest on 10% debentures as it does to pay dividend on $5\frac{1}{2}\%$ preference shares.

To illustrate the calculation, suppose company A issued £100,000 of 10% debentures and company B issued £100,000 of $5\frac{1}{2}\%$ preference shares. All other long-term capital was in ordinary shares, profits for both companies was £1 million, and corporation tax was 45%.

Company	A	B
	£100,000 in 10% debentures	£100,000 in 5½% preference shares
	£	£
Profit	1,000,000	1,000,000
Debenture interest (10%)	10,000	
	990,000	
45% corporation tax	445,500	450,000
	544,500	550,000
Preference dividend (5½%)	—	5,500
Available for equity	544,500	544,500

If market rate of interest for new debentures is 10% then 5½% may be said to be the break-even point for preference shares. Preference shares would clearly not be issued at more than 5½% if 10% debentures are possible, unless some other overriding consideration were taken into account.

The benefit accruing to the company in having debentures rather than preference shares is clearly recognized when companies like Trust Houses Group Ltd. redeem preference shares and issue debentures as replacements.

As with debentures, preference shares may be issued in perpetuity or they may have a specific redemption date.

Debentures

There are two main types of debenture, the mortgage debenture secured by the mortgage of particular property owned by the company, and the debenture with a floating charge. If the company goes into liquidation, mortgage debentures rank ahead of floating debentures up to the value of the secured property, and floating debentures rank ahead of any unsecured creditors. All creditors rank ahead of any shareholder.

The Savoy Hotel Ltd. has £700,000 8% mortgage debenture stock 1991/96 secured against the Savoy Hotel.

Most debenture issues are redeemable, that is repayable at or by a specified date, which may be effected

(a) By annual drawings out of profit.

(b) By the company purchasing its own debenture in the open market when the price is favourable.

(c) In a lump sum at maturity provided by means of a sinking fund. This method is considered in Volume 1. Examples of this method are to be found in the hotel and catering industry, for example:
Myddleton Hotels and Estates Limited. £400,000 7½% mortgage deben-

ture 1991 (year of redemption) in respect of which a sinking fund of £8,000 per annum started in 1971.

Debentures may be issued to named persons or made payable to bearer when they may be quoted on the Stock Exchange.

Convertible Debentures

Loan stock holders who have the right to convert their stock to ordinary shares at a future date or series of dates, hold convertible debentures, the final decision to convert resting with the debenture holder.

An advantage to the company compared with a redeemable debenture is that the debt is self-liquidating in that debentures are exchanged for ordinary shares and no funds are needed with which to redeem them.

Compared with an immediate ordinary share issue the convertible is cheaper in annual outgoings, which is helpful when required for a hotel development likely to take some time to build up to a profit earning stage.

An example is Grand Metropolitan Hotels. $6\frac{1}{2}\%$ convertible unsecured loan stock 1984/89.

Mortgages

A mortgage loan is one taken out against land or property and is similar in some ways to a secured debenture. However, differences between them include:

1. The interest rate of a mortgage cannot normally be fixed over the life of the agreement as is the interest on a debenture.
2. Regular payments of interest and principal are made to liquidate the loan which are usually for a shorter period of time than a debenture.
3. The mortgage holder has the first call on a company's assets in the event of a default in payment.

International Loans

Borrowing by British hotel groups extends to the international money market, in particular the Euro-dollar market which is the freest sector of this market. The market is so called because most of the banks accepting foreign currency deposits are in Europe, and such deposits are largely in U.S. dollars although they may be for instance pound sterling, the Swiss franc and the German mark.

Examples include Trust Houses Forte, and J. Lyons who in 1970 borrowed £2·5 million in Swiss francs over seven years at 9% for the first three years and subsequent rates to be based on inter-bank borrowing rates. This loan was used to replace short-term borrowings on bank overdraft. A loan of £5 million in Deutschmarks at an initial rate of $9\frac{1}{4}\%$ by Lyons in 1969 was said to be used for developments.

Special Finance Institutions

The Industrial and Commercial Finance Corporation Limited (I.C.F.C.) was set up in 1945 to assist the smaller concern requiring long-term loan or share capital. At 31st March, 1969, its investments in some 2,000 concerns totalling £102 million were divided as follows:

Loans	68%
Preference shares	15%
Ordinary shares	17%

The Estate Duties Investment Trust Limited (E.D.I.T.H.) was set up in 1952 in order to relieve the immediate problem of finding the finance for meeting estate duties while still allowing the private companies concerned to continue their separate existence. Holders of shares in family businesses and companies whose shares are privately held may be seriously affected by death duties which may lead to loss of control of a business.

Finance Without Initial Ownership

Financial arrangements of obtaining the use of capital facilities without ownership, open to the small and large firm alike, includes leasing, hire purchase, mortgaging and sale and lease back.

There is increasing awareness that two distinct decisions need to be made when obtaining long-term assets, one is to decide whether a particular asset is in fact required – an investment decision – and the other is the most appropriate means of obtaining the asset – a financial decision.

Leasing

This has been common for many years, for example internal telephones, and leasing companies provide virtually every industry with a convenient package deal if required. One lease can embrace complete furnishing of an hotel. The fundamental difference between leasing and other forms of finance is that title in the goods remains permanently vested in the 'lessor'. A lease comprises a primary period and a secondary period. During the primary period a rental commensurate with the cost of the equipment is paid by the lessee; the secondary period rentals are nominal. The total length of the lease is negotiated with the lessee but bears a relationship to the anticipated useful working life of the equipment; the normal primary periods are 3, 4 or 5 years' duration with 2, 6 or 5 year secondary periods respectively. The primary period rentals may be paid monthly, quarterly, half yearly or annually in advance.

Leasing offers a number of advantages to the lessee including:
1. It is the use of equipment, not its ownership, which is vital for profitability.
2. Use of equipment is gained on payment of first rental.
3. Working capital is left free for more profitable employment.
4. Rentals are fully tax-deductible.
5. Budgeting is facilitated.
6. Managers are more easily able to face up to obsolescence of existing plant and equipment because of ease of renewal.

The main reason for buying rather than leasing assets is perhaps that the cost is often higher to lease, although this depends upon the interest cost of raising money to make the purchase, or if money is available, the earnings which would be sacrificed in making the purchase.

Generally speaking the leasing company is content to receive a fair return on their money and to leave the larger share of earnings to the business prepared to use the asset and take the entrepreneurial risks.

Contract Hire
Contract hire is a form of leasing which is generally for shorter periods of time.

Hire Purchase
Hire Purchase may be the only means of acquiring certain assets. The purchaser makes a down payment or deposit and enters into a contract to hire goods for a specific time, say two years, making regular periodic payments for the hire, and at once acquires possession but not ownership of the goods. At the end of the hire period the hirer may purchase the goods outright for a small cash consideration, or the ownership may pass on the last payment. Although the most expensive of all credit facilities hire purchase is particularly useful since no security is needed though the hirer may be required to provide private legal and financial information and offer a guarantee.

Sale and Lease Back
Sale and lease back of property is a popular source of finance for hotel companies. Companies owning freehold properties or long leaseholds and having good profit records may benefit from selling such properties or leases to a finance or life assurance company for full market value and then lease back for a long term frequently, 99–120 years, at a rental directly related to the sale price, including cost of purchase, and would be in the range of $8\frac{1}{2}$–10%. Provision would be made during the course of the lease for upward rental review at intervals now normally of not more than 7 years. During the term of the lease the vendor would normally be responsible for maintaining and insuring the building.

Advantage to the vendor depends upon the use made of the money no longer tied up in the property. Inflation may add considerably to the rental and at the end of the long lease the vendor has no building as an asset. Many companies who have sold and leased back properties believe that with efficient management, monies released will earn a return which, having covered the rental, will provide a satisfactory dividend, allow for inflation, and still leave cash available for ploughing back. In short, many efficient managements consider this method of financing a profitable proposition.

A disadvantage might well be the effect on other sources of finance for instance where property is secured. Too high a proportion of leased properties might inhibit the issue of debentures for lack of security.

Hotels are particularly suitable candidates for sale and lease back transactions because the appreciation in value of the land encourages property and other finance companies to obtain regular revenue and a hedge against inflation, while hotel managements are able to use the funds so freed to take advantage of the tremendous expansion opportunities prevailing in the early 1970s. The

Post Houses are examples of financing by this source. In fact the capital programme of Trust Houses Forte group in 1970 was £20 million of which £10 million was lease-backs and £10 million ownerships.

Long-term Finance – Gearing (Leverage in U.S.A.)

The ideal capital structure for an expanding company is difficult to determine since it is largely a matter of opinion. The capital structure is measured by relating the medium- and long-term fixed interest capital to total capital employed. The company is said to be high geared if a large proportion of its capital is in fixed interest securities such as preference shares and debentures. Company gearing may be measured in a number of ways, a common method is

$$\frac{\text{fixed interest securities}}{\text{total capital employed}} \times 100$$

There is no ideal standard percentage, much depending upon the type of industry and whether fixed assets are owned or leased. What is important, however, is the effect on ordinary shareholders' earnings of increasing the gearing as shown in Exhibit 13–1 of two companies with opposite gearings:

Exhibit 13–1

	L.G. Ltd. *at 31/12/75*	*H.G. Ltd.* *at 31/12/75*
	£	£
Ordinary shares of £1	1,300,000	750,000
Debentures 10%	200,000	750,000
	1,500,000	1,500,000
Year ended	31/12/75	31/12/75
	£	£
15% return before interest	225,000	225,000
less 10% Debenture interest	20,000	75,000
Equity earnings before tax	205,000	150,000
less Corporation Tax (45%)	92,250	67,500
	112,750	82,500
Earnings per Share	£0·087	£0·110
Gearing	13·3%	50%
	(Low geared)	(High geared)

Because the rate of earnings before interest (15%) is greater than debenture interest rate itself (10%), ordinary shareholders benefit by the residue.

A high-geared company has extreme effects on ordinary shareholders' earnings. If H.G. Ltd. was successful in 1976 but failed in 1977 to the extent shown in Exhibit 13–2, the fortune of ordinary shareholders can be traced.

Exhibit 13–2

	H.G. Ltd. 31/12/76	H.G. Ltd. 31/12/77
Year ended		
Return on capital employed before interest	25%	5%
	£	£
Profit before interest	375,000	75,000
Less 10% Debenture interest	75,000	75,000
	300,000	nil
Less Corporation tax (45%)	135,000	
	165,000	
Earnings per share $\dfrac{£165,000}{750,000}$	$=£0.220$	nil

It may be seen that with return before interest on capital employed going up from £225,000 to £375,000 in 1976, an increase of 67%, equity earnings have risen by 100% from £0·110 to £0·220 per share because of high gearing. However, when low profits are earned the ordinary shareholders are worse off in a high geared company than a low geared one. H.G. Shareholders are left with no return when profit before interest drops to £75,000, whereas L.G. Shareholders

would have received	£75,000
less 10% interest	£20,000
	£55,000
less 45% Cpn. tax	£24,750
	£30,250

If a company is confident of its future prospects it should seek to maximize its gearing subject to limitations to ensure that it does not become over-geared. One guide is that the interest charge should be covered four times.

An efficiently financed industrial company should be able to raise up to 35% of its long-term capital needs in loan form. However, companies with much owned property because of good security are able to raise higher proportions of debt capital. Before their merger in 1970 Trust Houses had long-term debt amounting to 42% of its capital employed whilst Forte at 61·3% was even higher.

Takeovers and Mergers

Managements planning to expand operations can have new facilities built or buy existing facilities. The more usual means of expanding the smaller business, if local demand exists, is the purchase of adjoining premises, a method used by Mario Cassandro and Franco Lagattolla who started in 1959 with a capital of £1,200, earned as waiters. They opened a small trattoria in Soho and a few years later bought two adjoining buildings to start their development, through acquisition of restaurants, into a successful business valued at £1 million when it became a public company in 1968. Reasons for their success are said to be that they found a successful marketing formula and maintained a high standard without losing control of prices; found an understanding bank manager at the beginning; and got on well together and worked extremely hard.

Although a number of hotels have been built by Fortes, Sir Charles Forte prefers buying existing hotels because he reckons that from the turnover record one can better estimate potential turnover and profit, allowing very often for an increase in occupancy rate and catering turnover, and a reduction in wages content.

Expansion is designed to increase earnings per share of a business and buying hotels is a favourite means of achieving this growth. The blending of two or more existing undertakings into one undertaking goes under many names, the popular ones being takeovers and mergers. There is little difference between the two. The city code on takeovers and mergers aimed at protecting shareholders' interests never mentions one without the other.

Generally speaking however when the boards of directors of two companies agree to amalgamate in the interest of both, a merger is the right term. On the other hand a large company wanting to gain control of a smaller business whose board does not recommend the change, is said to be attempting to take over the smaller company.

Differences in corporate structure result from takeovers and mergers.

A takeover bid refers to an offer which may be made either to the whole of a company's shareholders or those owning ordinary shares, to purchase their existing stock holding at a price which is sufficiently over the current Stock Exchange quotation for the shares, so as to induce them to sell out in return for quoted shares in the bidding company, debentures, cash, or some combination of these. If the bid succeeds then the corporate identity of the business taken over may disappear.

A merger between two or more companies often results in a new company being created, and a reorganization of the capital structure takes place, for example Trust Houses and Forte in 1970 merged to become Trust Houses Forte group.

Takeovers
An undertaking which is seen not to be utilizing its resources to the full and whose management does not appear to be of the highest order, tends to be in danger of takeover for the simple reason that there is room for profit improvement under a more effective management. Underutilized resources may be cash, stocks, and fixed assets. The latter, for instance an hotel, may have a low bedroom occupancy rate which might be capable of improvement, and further, it may be owned when a sale and lease back transaction might be more profitable in releasing cash for further expansion.

Mr. Charles Clore was the best known of the financiers who brought to the attention of industry and shareholders alike the importance of under-used assets. His most successful take-over was of J. Sears & Co. (True-Form Boot Co.) owning 900 shops, several hundred of which he sold and leased back thereby gaining control of a good business and property worth more than £8 million for only £3 million. An unsuccessful bid of Mr. Clore's, but one which reminded the brewery industry that they owned valuable property which could raise cash, was for the Watney-Mann group. The bid did the group much good for they carried out a property re-organization themselves.

Mr. Clore developed a takeover technique which became standard practice. Having found a company under-using its assets – a suitable takeover candidate – he spent many months buying shares through a nominee name in the interests of secrecy. If he failed to obtain control by obtaining enough shares he still made a good profit because his action had forced the share prices up, the shares being undervalued in the first instance.

In the hotel world the Savoy Hotel Ltd. has long battled against being taken over, starting with Mr. Clore in 1953, when he obtained 10% of the equity. However Mr. Harold Samual, through his company Land Securities Investment Trust, was also interested and had over 20% of the equity. The plum was said to be the Berkeley Hotel and its site which could be more profitably used as offices and showrooms, although Savoy management, whilst admitting the hotel's unsatisfactory trading results, said to be caused by a decline in restaurant sales, had plans of their own to make the hotel more profitable. Mr. Clore sold his shares to Mr. Samual who now owned 30%. The Savoy directors realizing the threat of being taken over took legal steps to ensure that the target, the Berkeley, be safeguarded, resulting in Mr. Samual admitting defeat by selling his shares.

Seventeen years later the Savoy group was again under attack when Mr. Nigil Broackes, chairman of Trafalgar House Investments, bought over 18 months 10% of their shares, ostensibly to attempt a takeover.

Considerations of takeover situations indicate the separate functions of managing money – financial management – and managing business operations, and this becomes clear in the sale and lease back transaction. From an operational viewpoint it does not matter whether the facilities are owned or leased so long as there are no restrictions in the lease which affect operations. The decision to sell and lease back is essentially a financial one.

Mergers
Three categories can be determined:
1. Horizontal merger where both firms are doing the same kind of work, for instance hotels.
2. Vertical merger linking firms at immediately related stages of operations, for instance restaurants linking with prepackaged food production.
3. Conglomerate merger where activities of the firm are in entirely different spheres such as hotels and copying machine production and hire.

Some advantages of merging are savings in production, administration and selling costs, greater financial strength improving facilities for raising capital, economy in capital expenditure and current assets, greater market share improving and extending corporate image.

The Trust Houses Forte merger in 1970 was said to have benefited both companies in three ways:

1. Management skills and types of activity were complementary specializing between them in the related fields of hotels, catering and entertainment.
2. Geographically the two businesses were complementary.
3. The two companies were each too small to establish their own selling offices in major areas particularly abroad but merging made this possible.

It is probable that the first benefit of the Trust Houses Forte merger is the most important of any advantages through mergers in the industry, and the biggest disadvantage any subsequent loss of personal touch and individualism on the operations side, although modern marketing techniques should cope with this problem.

Company Amalgamations

Various methods of amalgamating are available to limited companies and the chosen method depends on considerations such as taxation, capital structures, share ownership and the marketing policy to be pursued.

The main forms of amalgamation are:

1. The creation of a new company which takes over the assets and liabilities of the merging companies which are wound up.
2. The creation of a new 'holding company' whereby the old companies continue their separate existence.
3. By absorption whereby the purchasing company takes over the whole of the assets and liabilities of the company which goes into liquidation.
4. Amalgamation by company A acquiring a controlling interest in company B whereby sufficient number of shares of company B are purchased.
5. Company A buys less than 51% of the voting shares in company B, both companies having common trade links. Company B is regarded as an associated company by A.

Valuing a Business

The purchase and sale of a business implies that a selling price has been agreed between the parties to the sale, the price normally being a negotiated one.

How will the business be valued to help determine price?

A business with quoted shares has a ready made basis of valuation, namely the quoted price on the Stock Exchange, but all other businesses must rely to some extent on accounting information such as the profit and loss account and balance sheet.

Goodwill

If the latest balance sheet, truly reflecting market values, showed a business to be worth £20,000 consisting of fixcd assets £15,000 and net current assets £5,000 and a buyer was prepared to pay £23,000 for it, he would be paying £3,000 for goodwill which had built up over the years. Certainly a business may be worth more than the value of its tangible assets because of good personal service provided or good location although the value representing such benefits does not appear in the balance sheet until the value materializes as the business changes hands.

Goodwill can be seen to be very much tied up with the value placed on a business when it is sold and is the difference between agreed purchase price and balance sheet values taken over.

Lord Macnaughton said of goodwill that it is the attractive force that brings in custom. It is the one thing which distinguishes an old established business from a new business at its first start.

The value of goodwill is what one can get for it. However, there are various methods used to evaluate goodwill so that at least a starting point may be found as a basis for negotiations.

(a) Super-profits. This value is based on the excess of a forecast profit on investment for from three to five years over average profit for the same period expected in the industry.

(b) Another method first values the business from forecast profit and then derives goodwill by deducting net asset value of the business. If profits were estimated to be £5,000 per annum and a 20% annual return were required, the buyer would be prepared to pay £25,000 ($\frac{100 \times £5,000}{20}$).

A net asset value of £20,000 would leave £5,000 for goodwill. If a 15% return were required, the price would rise to £33,333 and £13,333 would be paid for goodwill.

(c) A method which compares profits from buying the business with profit from alternative use of the purchase money is in line with modern decision making techniques, but its acceptance depends upon the quantification of alternative plans.

Assume that a restaurant was for sale in an area which fitted in with marketing policy and a buying price was required. At the same time a new restaurant could be built for the net asset value of the restaurant for sale.

Profits from the alternative investments are as follows:

End of Year	Estimated profits from restaurant for sale £	Estimated profits from new restaurant £
1	5,000	2,000
2	5,000	3,000
3	5,000	4,000
4	5,000	5,000
5	5,000	5,000

The amount of goodwill the buyer would be prepared to pay would be the net present value of the difference in the profits, discounting at the cost of capital to the buyer. In other words suppose the buyer had to borrow the purchase price at 10% per annum, what extra would he borrow to pay above the net asset value so as to make both investments of equal value?

The answer is £5,130 which can be proved in Exhibit 13–3, assuming profits and interest payable occur at the year end.

Exhibit 13–3

	Year End	Restaurant for Sale £	New restaurant £
Amount borrowed		25,130	20,000
Interest at 10%	1	2,513	2,000
		27,643	22,000
Profit reducing loan	1	5,000	2,000
		22,643	20,000
Interest at 10%	2	2,265	2,000
		24,908	22,000
Profit reducing loan	2	5,000	3,000
		19,908	19,000
Interest at 10%	3	1,992	1,900
		21,900	20,900
Profit reducing loan	3	5,000	4,000
		16,900	16,900

No further calculations are needed if profits from each investment are identical after year 3. Further calculations on the same line as the above using an annual profit figure of £5,000 would lead to the conclusion that the loan would be fully repaid about year 8.

If cost of capital is 10% then the restaurant valued at £25,130 with profits as stated is equal to £20,000 investment in a new restaurant with the smaller initial profits.

The actual calculations of the goodwill of £5,130 will be more fully understood after dealing with the topic of discounted cash flow in Chapter 15 where the calculation of £5,130 is made. (Exhibit 15–6.)

For the purpose of valuing a business when net asset value is taken into account, it is important that up-to-date values are used, for example an undervalued freehold property would benefit the purchaser unless the fact were taken into account when negotiating the sale.

Goodwill – Partnerships
Whilst goodwill can only appear in the books of a sole trader if a business has been purchased, the books of a partnership may also show goodwill created to compensate existing partners when a new partner is admitted.

Valuation of the Private Limited Company
The basic principle in share valuations is the determination of a fair price for the shares as between a willing buyer and a willing seller, the business being regarded as a going concern. There would be a close examination of the memorandum and articles, of the asset position as disclosed by the last balance sheet, and of the trading results of the period.
Valuation may be based on:
(a) Net tangible assets making allowances for undervalued property and suchlike, also goodwill.
(b) Forecast profits, when the value taken is so many years profit according to the industry.
The resulting valuation divided by the number of equity shares will give the share value required. Goodwill is simply the difference between balance sheet valuation and purchase price as described earlier.

Valuation of the Public Limited Company
The price officially quoted on the Stock Exchange forms a ready-made valuation of shares which is the basis of negotiations between potential buyer and seller.

Depreciation of Goodwill
Practice varies on this matter and businessmen may choose to write off goodwill or to maintain it as a permanent asset. Some companies show a nominal £1 goodwill in their accounts. The tendency is to write it down in years when good profits have been made.

Questions and Problems

13–1   Explain what is meant by the term 'gearing' and why certain companies in particular fields tend to be more highly geared than industry as a whole.

13–2   What advantage, if any, accrues to ordinary shareholders when a company issues debentures.

13–3   Why, under the present taxation system, are preference share issues out of favour, but debenture issues popular with company boards of directors? Illustrate with assumed figures.

13–4   A large hotel and catering company is considering raising additional capital for expansion. List the various forms of capital which are available, and give a brief description of each.   (H.C.I.M.A.)

13–5   A successful and expanding but relatively small private company, which owns two hotels and has a profit before tax of £45,000, finds its rate of growth restricted by lack of capital.

You are required to set out the advice which you would give as to how and where the company may obtain both additional working and fixed capital.

Assume such further facts concerning the company as are necessary for your answer.   (H.C.I.M.A.)

13–6   Explain some of the reasons for companies in the hotel and catering industry amalgamating.

13–7   Compare mergers with take-overs by discussing their similarities and differences.

13–8   Calculate goodwill on purchase of Company A, given the following information:

Company A

Forecast profit – Year	1	15,000
	2	20,000
	3	25,000

Net Assets valued at £100,000
Average return for the industry 15%
You are to use two methods known to you.

13–9   The Golden Restaurant is up for sale. The capital employed amounts to £20,000 and recent profits are:

1972 : £3,000	1975 : £4,000
1973 : £3,200	1976 : £3,700
1974 : £3,500	

The profits quoted do not include a figure for proprietor's salary which is reckoned to be about £1,500 p.a.

A close look at the accounts reveals that the 1975 figure included £300 exceptional income but the 1976 profit was determined after £800 had been written off, whereas £1,000 would have been a more reasonable figure.

The proprietor indicates that he wants the goodwill to be valued on the basis of 3 years' purchase of the average net profits for the past five years as shown in his accounts.

Assuming a reasonable return for this type of business is 10%, you should put forward your views as to which method ought to be the basis for negotiations.

Further Reading
1. Clarkson, G. P., and Elliot, B. J., *Managing Money and Finance*, Gower Press; chapters 9 to 13.
2. A.C.C.A., *Sources of Capital*.
3. A.C.C.A., *A Quotation for your Shares*.

CHAPTER FOURTEEN

SOURCE AND APPLICATION OF FUNDS

THE statement of source and application of funds or 'funds statement' is now established as an end of year statement alongside the balance sheet and profit and loss account. It provides a link between the balance sheet at the beginning of the year, the profit and loss account for the year and the balance sheet at the end of the year.

Control of profit performance and liquidity are two of the most important financial aspects of a successful business. Accounting emphasis has always been on profit and the many ways it may be defined and used for various purposes. Indeed the operating statement we have seen helps keep management aware of the profit performance of sections of the business whilst the profit and loss appropriation account shows, inter alia, how profit has been used. The growing importance placed upon the reporting of liquidity and changes in liquidity has led to the funds statement which is designed to show how movements in assets, liabilities and capital in a period have changed the company's net liquid fund position. Net liquid funds are defined as cash at bank and in hand and cash equivalents, e.g. investments held as current assets, less bank overdrafts and other borrowings repayable within one year of the accounting date.

Enterprises with turnover or gross income of £25,000 and over are recommended to include a funds statement as part of their audited accounts for periods beginning on or after 1st January, 1976.[1]

Explanation of Funds

A funds statement is prepared from Balance Sheets at the beginning and end of a period taking account also of further information available in the Profit and Loss Account and elsewhere. First it must be understood what items are regarded as sources of funds and application of funds, secondly a format for presentation is necessary into which each item may be slotted, and thirdly the object of the statement should always be borne in mind, that is to show how net liquid funds (cash and equivalents) have been generated and absorbed by the operations of the business in the period.

To help in the initial understanding, an example follows consisting of:

(*a*) Basic data – being a summary of a first year's operations. (Exhibit 14–1)
(*b*) Notes on the data.
(*c*) The resulting funds statement. (Exhibit 14–2)

Statement of Standard accounting practice (SSAP) No. 10.

This approach has been chosen because with no starting balance sheet, the end of period figures given reflect changes in the period, which makes for simplicity.

A further example is used (Exhibit 14–3) to show the more usual situation of preparing a funds statement from balance sheets at two points in time. Here further aspects are developed.

Exhibit 14–1

Summary of first year's operations

Note references	£000	Source of funds £000	Application of funds £000
(a) Cash from share issue		100	
(b) Equipment bought for cash			60
(c) Sales	600		
Expenses (excluding depreciation)	560		
Cash from operations	40 ——→	40	
Depreciation	10		
Profit from operations	30		
(d) Debtors increase			20
(e) Creditors increase		30	
(f) Stocks increase			40
(g) Tax provision		10	
(h) Dividends paid			10
(i) Cash balances (increase)			40
		170	170

Notes on first year's operations

(a) Cash from debentures is similarly a source. Any premium obtained is an additional source. Cash paid to redeem debentures will be an application.

(b) Cash from the sale of fixed assets will be a source. Profit or loss on sale is disregarded.

(c) Cash from operations is not strictly correct as a description because £20,000 is still outstanding as Debtors increase. However, it is called in the funds statement funds 'generated from operations'.

Depreciation does not provide cash for replacing fixed assets which lose value. It is not a cash transaction but merely an accounting entry apportioning a part of the historical cost to an accounting period.

(d) Debtors increase is an application because cash has been sacrificed. If debtors decreased, cash will have flowed in, the amount of the decrease being a source of funds.

(e) Creditors represent a short term source of funds.

(f) Stocks increase means that money has been diverted to build up stocks, an application of funds. When stocks are unnecessarily high, their reduction provides cash by avoiding having to purchase so much for operations.

(g) Provisions and reserves do not involve movement of cash and are therefore, neither source nor application of funds. Tax paid in a period however, is an application of funds.

(h) In the same way as the treatment of Tax, dividends are taken into the statement when they are paid.

(i) An increase in the cash balance, like any other asset increase, is an application of funds. A bank overdraft is clearly recognized as a source of funds.

Exhibit 14–2

Statement of Source and Application of Funds[1]
Year 1977

	£000	£000
Source of funds		
Profit before tax		30
Adjustments for items not involving movement of funds:		
Depreciation		10
Total generated from operations		40
Funds from other sources		
Issue of shares for cash		100
		140
Application of funds		
Dividends paid	(10)	
Purchase of fixed assets	(60)	(70)
		70
Increase/decrease in working capital		
Increase in stocks	(40)	
Increase in debtors	(20)	
Increase in creditors – excluding taxation and proposed dividends	30	
Movement in net liquid funds:		
Cash balances	(40)	(70)

[1]Symbols: ( )=application of funds. Other figures are sources.

Funds Statement Preparation

There are two methods of preparing a funds statement from two balance sheets and additional internal information, a short cut method and a longer systematic method. The first method will be demonstrated and the second shown in outline. Information available are the balance sheets and three notes as follows:

Balance Sheets at 31st March

	1978 £000	1977 £000
ASSETS		
Fixed assets at cost	240	220
Depreciation	14	12
	226	208
Current assets:		
Stocks	55	40
Debtors	35	20
Bank and cash balances	10	30
	326	298
LIABILITIES		
Issued share capital	150	150
Revenue reserves	40	30
Retained profits	16	18
Loan capital	60	40
Current liabilities:		
Creditors	36	38
Current taxation	8	7
Proposed dividends	16	15
	326	298

Notes:
1. Equipment was purchased for £60,000.
2. Equipment was sold for £41,000. Depreciation of £5,000 was included in £12,000 charged to 1977. Original cost was £40,000.
3. £10,000 was transferred to revenue reserves in 1978.

Shortcut method
1. Draft the main headings of a funds statement leaving plenty of space under each heading.
2. Any balance sheet differences which need no adjustment are inserted in statement. This will take account of loan capital, creditors, taxation paid,

dividends paid, stocks, debtors, bank and cash balances. Tax and dividends are the 1977 current liabilities assumed to have been paid in 1978.
3. Use the above notes to determine further items such as equipment purchases and sales.
4. Completion of the statement requires the calculation of depreciation for the year if this is not supplied. To insert totals simple deduction is used. Increase in working capital of £12,000 added to other application of funds totalling £82,000 gives £94,000 which is the total source. Total generated from operations is the sum of funds from other sources taken away from total sources giving £33,000. Depreciation deducted from this figure gives profit before tax.

Exhibit 14–3

Statement of Source and Application of Funds
Year 1978

	£000	£000
Source of funds		
Profit before tax		26
Depreciation		7
		—
Total generated from operations		33
Funds from other sources		
Loan capital		20
Sale of equipment		41
		—
		94
Application of funds		
Tax paid	(7)	
Dividend paid	(15)	
Purchase of equipment	(60)	(82)
	—	—
		12
Increase/decrease in working capital		
Increase in stocks	(15)	
Increase in debtors	(15)	
Decrease in creditors	(2)	
Movement in net liquid funds:		
Bank and cash balances	20	(12)
	—	═══

5. The advantage of speed in preparation must be weighed against the chance of errors creeping in which would make the balancing figure of profit inaccurate. If, however, the profit and loss account is to hand then this creates no problem for the profit before tax figure – the important first item in the

statement – is available. The reconstructed account for this example is as follows:

Appropriation Section of the Profit and Loss Account
for the year to 31st March 1978

	£		£
Tax provision	8,000	Unappropriated profit from 1977	18,000
Proposed dividend	16,000	Profit on equipment sale[1]	6,000
Transfer to Reserve	10,000	Balancing item = Profit before	
Balance c/d	16,000	tax (1978)	26,000
	£50,000		£50,000

Systematic Method

This method ensures a balanced statement by starting with columns for balance sheet differences and applying adjustments which are self-balancing. The adjustments are to take account of sale of fixed assets and of profit and loss account items so that one is left with profit before tax and depreciation.

Exhibit 14-4

Balance sheet items	Balance sheet differences		Adjustments		Final figures for statement	
	Source	Application	Source	Application	Source	Application
	£000	£000	£000	£000	£000	£000
ASSETS						
Fixed assets at cost		20		+40(b)		60(f)
Depreciation	2		+5(c)		7	
Stocks		15				15
Debtors		15				15
Cash	20				20	
LIABILITIES						
Shares						
Revenue reserves	10		+16(e)	+6(d) ⎫	26	
Retained profit		2	+8(e)	⎬		
Loan capital	20			⎭	20	
Creditors		2				2
Current tax	1			+8(e)		7
Proposed dividends	1			+16(e)		15
	54	54				
Fixed asset sale			+41(a)		41	
			+70	+70	114	114

[1]Normally profit or loss on sale of assets will feature in the main body of the profit and loss account.

Notes:
(*a*) Cash from equipment sale.
(*b*) Original cost of sale item.
(*c*) Depreciation of sale item.
(*d*) Profit on sale added back.
(*e*) Tax dividends (current liabilities) added back.
(*f*) Resulting figure is cost of purchase.

Review
Only one form of presentation has been used in this chapter to avoid confusion. However, a wide variety of forms are encountered in practice ranging from one which simply lists and totals the sources and applications, to one which may start with the opening net liquid funds and end with the equivalent closing balance. The tendency is to highlight favourable aspects, and the latter form might be used where the improvement in net liquid funds may be negligible whilst the opening and closing balances might each be significantly large. The minimum amount of 'netting off' of say purchase and sale of fixed assets is recommended although some 'netting off' may be inevitable through the lack of information. In published accounts the funds statement should show figures for both the period under review and for the previous period.

Relationships between individual sources and applications can sometimes be recognised such as a long term loan raised in the period providing funds to expand shown as the purchase of fixed assets and increases in stocks and debtors.

Finally a statement of source and application of funds, or funds statement for short, is important as a budget taking its place beside the budgeted balance sheet as an indication of the financial policy of the enterprise.

Questions and Problems
14–1   Describe the meaning of the terms 'cash flow' and 'profit' and explain their differences.

14–2   Indicate by a tick whether each of the following financial changes effect a cash inflow, outflow or no change:

Financial change	Cash inflow	Cash outflow	No effect on cash
Share capital issue			
Decrease in creditors			
Sale of investments			
Annual depreciation charge			
Loan repayment			
Decrease in debtors			
Increase in general reserve			
Increase in stock			
Goodwill written off			
Decrease in cash			
Purchase of fixed assets			

14-3   It is sometimes desirable to ascertain from the balance sheet how changes
       in the liquid resources of a limited company have arisen.
       List the factors which may have caused:
       (*a*) A decrease in the liquid position
       (*b*) An increase in the liquid position.

14-4   Is it possible for a company to achieve a net profit in a period and yet
       show a net cash outflow?

14-5   The annual accounts of the Aldo Hotel Co. Ltd. are as follows:

Balance Sheet as at 31st May, 1976

1975 £000		£000	1975 £000		£000
80	Authorized and issued capital	80	170	Fixed assets – at cost	180
5	Reserves	10	10	Additions in year at cost	40
			180		220
10	Unappropriated profits	8	99	Less depreciation	105
–	Loan	12			
			81		115
			9	Cash	2
15	Current liabilities	30	20	Other current assets	23
110		140	110		140

Profit and Loss Account (including appropriations)
for the year ended 31st May, 1976

8	Directors' remuneration	10	14	Profit b/d	20
4	Depreciation	6	8	Unappropriated profits b/f	10
–	Loan interest	1			
–	Transfer to reserves	5			
10	Unappropriated profits c/f	8			
22		30	22		30

You are required to:
(*a*) Prepare a source and application of funds statement reconciling
      the cash at bank at 1 June, 1975 with the cash at bank at 31st May,
      1976;
(*b*) Compare and contrast the information which can be established from

the annual accounts above with that in your source and application of funds statement for the Aldo Hotel Co. Ltd.   (H.C.I.M.A.)

14–6 The following is the balance sheet of the Silver Lining Hotel Ltd. for the year ended 30th April 1975:

SILVER LINING HOTEL LTD.
Balance Sheet as at 30th April, 1975

£ 1974	£	£		£ 1975	£
			Fixed assets		
500,000			Freehold hotel at valuation		500,000
	80,000		Equipment at cost	100,000	
	45,000		less depreciation	40,000	
35,000					60,000
535,000					560,000
			less working capital deficit current assets:		
	90,000		stocks	130,000	
	35,000		debtors	50,000	
	8,000		bank	—	
	133,000			180,000	
			Less current liabilities		
		79,000	Creditors 110,000		
		71,000	Corporation tax 60,000		
		—	Overdraft 50,000		
	150,000			220,000	
17,000					40,000
518,000			Net assets		520,000
			Represented by		
			Shareholders' Interest		
400,000			Issued share capital		400,000
60,000			Reserves		60,000
58,000			Unappropriated profit		60,000
518,000					520,000

Movements on the equipment account during the year were:

	1974	Sold	Purchases	Depn. charge	1975
Cost	80,000	30,000	50,000	—	100,000
Depn.	45,000	20,000	—	15,000	40,000
	35,000	10,000			60,000
Sale proceeds		4,000			
Loss charged to profit		6,000			

You are required to prepare:
- (*i*) a source and application of funds statement reconciling the opening cash at bank with the closing overdraft; and
- (*ii*) a critical report on your source and application statement and the balance sheet.   (H.C.I.M.A.)

14–7   The summarized balance sheets of the Alpine Post House at 31st March, 1972 and 1973 are below:

	1972 £	1973 £
Issued share capital	200,000	230,000
Share premium	20,000	22,000
Capital reserves	35,000	35,000
Retained profits	17,000	28,000
7½% convertible loan stock	50,000	30,000
8½% mortgage debentures	40,000	64,000
Trade creditors	8,000	11,000
Overdraft	34,000	—
Corporation tax	3,000	4,000
Proposed dividends	11,000	15,000
	418,000	439,000

	£	£
Freehold land and building at cost	216,000	216,000
Equipment, furniture and fittings (net)	134,000	140,000
Investment at cost	60,000	29,000
Food and beverage stocks	4,000	10,000
Trade debtors	2,000	6,000
Cash at bank and in hand	2,000	38,000
	418,000	439,000

Additional information:

- (*a*) Of the £30,000 increase in issued share capital, £20,000 had been in respect of the 7½% convertible loan stock.
- (*b*) Corporation tax figures shown are payable early the following year.
- (*c*) During the year furniture which had cost £12,000 had been sold for £900. Seven-eighths of its useful life had been written off. New equipment had been purchased for £22,000.

The net closing balances on equipment, furniture and fittings are made up as follows:

| | 1972 | 1973 |
	£	£
Balances at cost	180,000	190,000
Accumulated depreciation	46,000	50,000
	134,000	140,000

(*d*) During the year investments which had cost £31,000 had been sold for £35,000.

You are required to prepare a statement accounting for the cash increase that has occurred during the financial year ended 31st March, 1973.

(H.C.I.M.A.)

Further Reading

1. Accounting Standards Committee (A.S.C.), Statement of Standard Accounting Practice (S.S.A.P.) No. 10.

CHAPTER FIFTEEN

APPRAISING LONG-TERM INVESTMENTS

A BUSINESS must earn profits over a period of years to be at all successful, short-term gains sometimes having to be sacrificed in the interests of long-term goals. What are these long-term goals? They may be a combination of growth, security, even survival, but profitability is of such importance that where a business is faced with a choice between profit and some other goal, profit is usually preferred because survival depends upon it.

Opportunities for Achieving Long-term Goals

A successful business must recognize opportunities which might lead to a profitable long-term investment and the larger the firm the more important it is to seek out and find opportunities by applying some or all of the following:

(a) Forceful management with the persistence and personality to push forward proposals if they are considered viable.

(b) Appointment of staff to seek and find opportunities.

(c) Contacts with other bodies who could stimulate recognition of opportunities – trade associations, firms, etc.

(d) Procedures for producing statistics relating to changes in the activity of customers and competitors.

(e) Procedures to show changes in the balance between market demand and facilities available to meet it – leading to long-term forecasts.

Capital Investment

Whether the opportunity involves building a new hotel, modernizing an old one, or extending an hotel, money must be made available and spent on what might be called a 'Capital Investment' – that is expenditure incurred now in order to produce a stream of benefits over a period of years which will, it is hoped, result in the firm being in a more favourable position. Capital investment decisions differ from operating decisions by reason of the nature of the expenditure and the length of time before the full effect of the decision is felt.

Merrett and Sykes open their book[1] on the subject by stating 'the selection and financing of capital projects are indisputably two of the most important and critical business decisions'.

Savage and Small in their book[2] state 'probably the most important decision which any management has to take is the decision to invest'.

[1] *The Finance and Analysis of Capital Projects.*
[2] *Introduction to Managerial Economics.*

Wright states in his book[3] 'probably the most significant factor affecting the level of profitability in a business is the quality of the management's decisions relating to the commitment of the company's resources to new investment within the business'.

In order to formalize data associated with a project it is likely that the larger business would produce a 'feasibility study' which involves collecting and assembling information in terms of physical quantities and money. It will become an 'economic feasibility study' when there is included an appraisal of the project in terms of return on capital invested.

The study will include all information bearing on the project such as:

Marketing forecasts	– potential customers of varying categories showing basis of forecast – jumbo jets, etc.,
Additional physical facilities	– numbers of rooms of each kind, style of hotel, site, bar, games room, petrol station, etc.,
Government regulations	– planning permission, access, etc.,
Competition	– existing and forecast
Appraisal of project in financial terms	– taxation, inflation, etc.

Measuring Investment Returns

Bearing in mind the significance of a capital investment decision, care should be used in assessing the worth of proposed projects, and a simple example is here used to compare available evaluation methods.

A company with £1,116 available to invest is considering the following capital project, which after writing off depreciation of £279 per annum over its four-year life, shows forecast profits of:

Proposed project 123

	£
31st December, 1978	121
31st December, 1979	121
31st December, 1980	121
31st December, 1981	121
	484

Average annual profit on investment method

This is simply the average annual profit as a percentage of investment, in this case:

$$\frac{£121}{£1,116} \times 100 = 10 \cdot 8 \%$$

[3] *Discounted Cash Flow.*

For short-term investments of up to two years' duration this method might provide a reasonable basis for assessing their worth to the business, but the longer the period of the investment the less satisfactory the method becomes. The concern in this chapter will be with investments of longer than two years' duration in order to emphasize the importance of using the most appropriate method of assessment. Nevertheless, once the virtues of the appropriate method have been established, it can be seen to apply to all investment projects whether of short or long duration.

There are two serious limitations to the average annual profit on investment method.

(a) The resultant percentage is too imperfect to be of real value in assessing whether the investment should be accepted as a profitable one. Where profits are constant per annum, the percentage will always err on the low side and profitable projects may thus be rejected.

(b) In comparisons between competing projects the resultant percentage could easily favour the least profitable one because the method takes no account of the timing of profits and cash flows.

Average annual return on average investment
This is a variation of the first method in so far as only half the original investment is related to the average annual profit. Since the investment is worthless after four years, the average investment over the period is opening+closing investment÷2.

$$\frac{£1,116+£0}{2}=£558$$

The average return on £1,116 is 21·7%, double the first method.

The resultant percentage for a project with constant annual profits is always an optimistic figure.

Discounted cash flow technique
This takes into account the fact that as cash is received it is available for reducing the investment itself or for further investment, in the one case saving interest and in the other, gaining interest for the business. Profit each year must be converted to cash flow, which is a matter of adding back depreciation. Therefore in the example, £121 + £279 = £400 cash flow inwards each year.

Suppose the £1,116 were borrowed at 16% interest, payable on the balance outstanding at the end of each year, and that as cash comes in it is used to repay the loan. The result would be:

			£
1/1/78	Loan		1,116
31/12/78	Interest payable on loan outstanding at 16%	+	179
			1,295
	Repayment	−	400
			895
31/12/79	Interest payable at 16%	+	143
			1,038
	Repayment	−	400
			638
31/12/80	Interest payable at 16%	+	102
			740
	Repayment	−	400
			340
31/12/81	Interest payable at 16%	+	54
			394
	Repayment completing repayment of loan	−	400
		−	6 (negligible difference)

This indicates that it cost 16% to borrow the cash for the investment which provided the £400 per annum cash inflows and the interest paid had swallowed up all the proceeds, leaving no profit for the firm. But at the other extreme, if the investment cost the company nothing at all, then the cash return equals 16% over the period and the project produces a profit of 16%. More likely, however, the investment might cost anything between 0% and 16%, leaving some profit for the company.

Ignoring cost – which the average annual return does anyway – the project's true return of 16% compares with 10·8% and 21·7% of the first two methods.

To calculate the 16% in the normal way cash flows are discounted as in Exhibit 15–1, which is explained later.

Comparing Competing Projects

It is clearly better to receive £400 in cash now than in three years' time, even in one year's time, because of the opportunity afforded of reinvesting the cash over the interim period. Suppose another project (X47) was available to use up the £1,116 capital, and both projects' cash flows were as follows:

Cash flows

	Project 123		Project X47	
	In	Out	In	Out
	£	£	£	£
1/1/78		1,116		1,116
31/12/78	400		NIL	
31/12/79	400		400	
31/12/80	400		400	
31/12/81	400		800	
	1,600	1,116	1,600	1,116
Less investment	1,116		1,116	
Total profit	484		484	
Average annual profit	121		121	

Both projects would give a 10·8% return based on the average annual return method, favouring neither. By merely inspecting the cash flows, Project 123 can be seen to be worth more than X47 because the £400 receivable 31/12/78 on 123 is available for three years until 31/12/81 when the other project's cash flow catches up. If £400 were invested at 16% per annum with interest undrawn (compound interest) the £400 would accumulate to be worth £624 on 31/12/81, the interest being £224. This gives some idea of the difference in value of the projects when interest is considered.

The orthodox way of taking interest into account in investment projects is to eliminate the compound interest from cash flows and bringing them all down to a common value at the present moment in time – when the cash is invested. Therefore by discounting (the opposite of compounding interest) both projects' cash flows at the same rate of interest, they are reduced to a present value for easy comparison. Present value (p.v.) factors are available as tables[4] and they simply eliminate the interest factor. Exhibit 15–1 shows the calculation for each project. It will be noted that the discounted inflows exactly equal the outflow and the net present value @ 16% is nil, indicating that this is the D.C.F. return on the project. With project X47 the discounted inflows are £124 less than the outflow (investment) indicating the return to be less than 16%. But why is the difference in value of the projects only £124 when discounting is used, but £224 when the £400 cash flow difference is invested at 16% compound interest? Discounting has been said to be the reverse of adding compound interest, and this is true because each sum is at a different point in time:

£124   at   1/1/78
£224   at   31/12/81

[4]For present value table, see page 219.

a difference of four years. They must be at the same point in time for proper comparison, so that £124 with compound interest @ 16% = £224, and £224 discounted (multiplied by present value factor for 4 years of 0·55) = £124.

Exhibit 15–1

Statement comparing Project 123 with x47
on a Discounted Cash Flow Basis

Year	Date	123					X47				
		Cash flow		P.V. factor	Discounted Cash flows		Cash flow		P.V. factor	Discounted Cash flows	
		In	Out	16%	In	Out	In	Out	16%	In	Out
		£	£		£	£	£	£		£	£
0	1st Jan., '78		1,116	1·00		1,116		1,116	1·00		1,116
1	31st Dec., '78	400		0·86	344		—		0·86	—	
2	31st Dec., '79	400		0·74	296		400		0·74	296	
3	31st Dec., '80	400		0·64	256		400		0·64	256	
4	31st Dec., '81	400		0·55	220		800		0·55	440	
		1,600	1,116		1,116	1,116	1,600	1,116		992	1,116
					1,116					1,116	
Net Present Value of projects at 16%					Nil					−124	

Discounting: Compound Interest in Reverse

To demonstrate this approach to an understanding of D.C.F., the compound interest formula is introduced and then the discounting formula is seen to be the reverse of it.

Date	31st Dec. 78	31st Dec. 79	31st Dec. 80	31st Dec. 81
Calculation of interest at 16%	—	$£400 \times \frac{16}{100}$	$£464 \times \frac{16}{100}$	$£538.24 \times \frac{16}{100}$
Interest	—	£64	£74.24	£86.12
Investment value	£400	£464	£538.24	£624.36 (say £624)

It can be said that £400 'accumulates' to £624 which is the 'future worth' of £400 at 16% for three years; also that £624 receivable after three years 'discounts' at 16% to £400 'present value'.

The formula for calculating this 'compound interest' of £224 is:

$$S = P(1+r)^n$$

where
S = the future worth
P = the present value
r = the rate of return or interest
n = the number of periods

Substituting, we have $S = £400 (1 + \cdot 16)^3 = £624$
Therefore the compound interest is £224.

Present Value

The present value is seen to be compound interest in reverse and can be derived by reversing the formula for compound interest. The formula for calculating the present value of an amount receivable at some future time is therefore $P = \dfrac{S}{(1+r)^n}$ and substituting, $P = \dfrac{£624}{(1 \cdot 16)^3} = £400$. Alternatively, the present value of £1 can be calculated and multiplied by the amount which is to be reduced to present value. The present value of £1 is known as the present value factor or discount factor.

The present value of £1 at 16% receivable in 1 year's time is	$\dfrac{£1}{(1 \cdot 16)^1}$	=	£0·86207
receivable in 2 years' time is	$\dfrac{£1}{(1 \cdot 16)^2}$	=	£0·74316
receivable in 3 years' time is	$\dfrac{£1}{(1 \cdot 16)^3}$	=	£0·64066
receivable in 4 years' time is	$\dfrac{£1}{(1 \cdot 16)^4}$	=	£0·55229

The present value of £624·36 receivable 3 years hence at 16% is therefore £624·36 × 0·64066 = £400.

Present value of an annuity

When constant period cash flows are forecast a short-cut method of discounting is advised. The P.V. factors are summed and multiplied once by the constant cash flow. Project 123 (Exhibit 15–1) would be discounted by this method:

$$£400 (0 \cdot 86 + 0 \cdot 74 + 0 \cdot 64 + 0 \cdot 55)$$
$$= £400 \times 2 \cdot 79 = £1,116$$

The constant cash flow has the same characteristic as an annuity in that a sum of money is paid or received yearly during a specified time. A table is often available which shows the present value of the annuity of £1 for n periods, which simply saves the effort of adding P.V. factors. An extract from the 16% column of an annuity table would read:

1 year 0·86 more precisely 0·86207
2 years 1·60   1·60523
3 years 2·24   2·24589
4 years 2·79   2·79818

D.C.F. Methods

Net Present Value method

This method is used when it is required to determine whether a project is expected to exceed a particular percentage return set by management. If 16% was the minimum return a firm would accept from a new project, the discounting at this rate of proposed projects 123 and X47 in Exhibit 15–1 reveals 123 to be right on 16%, but X47 to be less than 16% because discounted inflows fall short of outflows.

Yield or Internal Rate of Return method

If management required to know the rate a project is expected to achieve, a project's cash flows are discounted at various rates until the rate is found which discounts inflows to equal outflows. A lucky guess might find the right rate straightaway like project 123 at 16%. However, X47 is known to be less than 16%. If a lower discount rate is used, and the inflows and outflows do not coincide, the true rate may be found by the use of ratios.
    For example:

Investment £1,116

	Cash inflows £	16% factors	£	10% factors	£
Year 1	—	0·86	—	0·91	—
2	400	0·74	296	0·83	332
3	400	0·64	256	0·75	300
4	800	0·55	440	0·68	544
			992		1,176
Less outflow (investment)			1,116		1,116
Net present value (N.P.V.)			− 124		+ 60

The position may be shown:

```
        ←— — — — — — — — — — —→
                 Range of 6%
Rate     10%          ?           16%

N.P.V.   £ +60        £0          £ − 124
                 Range of £184
        ←— — — — — — — — — — —→
```

The difference in rates used is 6% (16% −10%)
The difference in N.P.V. is the addition of £124 and £60 = £184.
The rate to add to 10% so that N.P.V. = £0 is:

$$\frac{£60}{£184} \times 6\% = 2\%.$$

Therefore the D.C.F. rate of return, the true rate is 12%.

A lucky choice would have been 12% in the first instance, e.g.

	Cash inflows £	12% factors	£
Year 1	—	0·89	—
2	400	0·80	320
3	400	0·71	284
4	800	0·64	512
			1,116
Less outflow (investment)			1,116
N.P.V. @ 12%			nil

Basic D.C.F. Considerations

1. Assumptions made in simple appraisal of projects giving adequate results are:
   (a) Cash flow inwards is on the last day of the period, although in practice it is a daily process.
   (b) Investment is reckoned to be at the beginning of the period, sometimes taken as Year 0 when no discounting is required.
2. Taxation may have a marked effect on the results of an appraisal and should be estimated for each project.
3. Inflationary effects should be considered if income and costs are not expected to rise in step with each other.
4. Most capital projects involve investment in working capital which must be regarded as a cash flow outwards once only when the increased level of working capital is required. Similarly it should be regarded as cash flow inwards when the project is expected to end.
5. Benefits obtained by using Discounted Cash Flow technique in judging proposed projects tend to be twofold. Firstly a more consistent financial appraisal is produced, and secondly the discipline in calculating after tax cash flows on an annual basis means that more care is likely to be exercised, an important consideration when so much is generally at stake.
6. The use of discounting techniques is only an aid to decision making. In the same way that control figures are no substitute for good supervision, so D.C.F. calculations are no substitute for a well prepared forecast of financial matters concerning a proposed project.

D.C.F. Example

Golden Hotels Ltd. are considering purchasing a suitable site and having an hotel built on it. A feasibility study shows the following figures: Cost of site and building £100,000, furniture and fittings £80,000, working capital £1,400, making a total initial investment of £181,400. Ten years has been considered as a reasonable life before drastic alterations require to be made, and after this time the building site is expected to be worth about £80,000 and the working capital will be regarded as no longer required. The net cash flows after tax each year are shown in the working statement. The cost of capital to the company is 6% and the return after tax on capital employed for the business is planned to be not less than 10%. The following is a summarized statement prepared to show whether the project meets the minimum criterion of 6% and the minimum planned rate of 10%. Inflation factors have been ignored. The present value factors are given to 3 decimal places. Tables are available which give 5 decimal places, but for most purposes 2 decimal places are accurate enough.

Payback Method of Appraisal (PB)

Payback period is defined as the number of years it takes for an investment to generate sufficient cash to recover its initial capital outlay in full. Its popularity is mainly due to its simplicity of application. Other reasons for its use are:

(a) A business with liquidity problems will be aided in the short term if projects with low PB periods are preferred.

(b) Using a low PB period it is said to reflect a dynamic management who want quick returns.

(c) It allows for a special type of risk which will bring the cash flow to a halt, such as foreign intervention or sudden competition.

Its chief draw-back is that it takes no account of the project's overall earnings or of the significance of cash flows within the PB period. It is not therefore a measure of profitability because one project might have a rating of two years and be unprofitable with no further net cash inflows whereas another project may have a three year PB period with high net cash inflows for another three years.

The payback period for project 123 is calculated as follows:

Year	Outflow £	Inflow £	Cumulative £
0	(1,116)	—	(1,116)
1	—	400	(716)
2	—	400	(316) (a)
3	—	400 (b)	84

$$\text{Payback} = 2 \text{ years} + \frac{a}{b} = 2 + \frac{316}{400} = 2 \cdot 79 \text{ years}$$

The period would be stated as 2·8 years or nearly 3 years.

It should be noted that it would be inadvisable to be too precise as the data on which the period is based – the cash flows – are themselves uncertain.

Exhibit 15–2

GOLDEN HOTELS LTD

PROPOSED PROJECT x50

Year	Notes	Cash Flow inwards (profit before depreciation and after tax) £	Present value factor at 6%	Discounted at 6% £	Present value factor at 10%	Discounted at 10% £
1 1978		5,000	0·943	4,715	0·909	4,545
2 1979		20,000	0·890	17,800	0·826	16,520
3 1980		20,000	0·840	16,800	0·751	15,020
4 1981		20,000	0·792	15,840	0·683	13,660
5 1982	(£22,000 less £1,000 furniture)	21,000	0·747	15,687	0·621	13,041
6 1983		23,000	0·705	16,215	0·564	12,972
7 1984	(£23,000 less £2,000 carpets)	21,000	0·665	13,965	0·513	10,773
8 1985		23,000	0·627	14,421	0·467	10,741
9 1986		23,000	0·592	13,616	0·424	9,752
10 1987		23,000	0·558	12,834	0·386	8,878
	Residual value £80,000 / Working capital 1,400	81,400	0·558	45,421	0·386	31,420
				187,314		147,322
	Less: Investment in Year 0 (beginning of year 1)			181,400		181,400
	NET PRESENT VALUE at 6%			+5,914		
	NET PRESENT VALUE at 10%					−34,078

Notes: 1. The table indicates that the rate of return is just over 6%, 6·59% by interpolation and falls well short of the rate of 10% that the company is looking for from its future enterprises. On financial grounds the project, as it stands, would be rejected.
2. Using P.V. factors to two decimal places the rate would be 6·61%, a negligible difference.

Further D.C.F. Considerations

Taxation
After-tax cash flows should be used in D.C.F. calculations because tax payments constitute an outflow of cash, and competing projects may have different tax allowances and charges which might influence the investment decision.

The following procedure is used for converting pre-tax cash flows to post-tax cash flows.

1. Determine the investment incentives available for the purchase. E.g. (*a*) Plant and machinery which includes office furniture, attracts 100% First Year Allowance. (*b*) Motor cars attract a Writing Down Allowance of 25% of cost in year of purchase and then a written down value in subsequent years. There is however, a maximum allowance per year.
2. The allowances are deducted from the pre-tax cash flow (profit + depreciation) leaving a figure of taxable profit.
3. When the plant is disposed of, any residual revenue is shown as cash inflow, and the writing down allowance in the final year adjusted (called the balancing allowance or balancing charge) so that capital allowances in total equal net cost of the asset (original cost less residual revenue).
4. Corporation tax is chargeable on each year's taxable profit and on average reckoned to be paid 12 months later.
5. Post-tax cash flows which come in for discounting consist of pre-tax cash flows less tax paid.
6. It is usually assumed that there are profits being generated elsewhere in the company against which capital allowances may be offset. Therefore a cash inflow of tax may be recorded in respect of a project where insufficient profit is made on it to absorb tax allowances.
7. If no profits are available in the company to use up capital allowances they may be carried forward until such time as there are profits available against which to set the allowances.

The following is an example of the above procedure.

Exhibit 15–3
The AB Hotel Group are considering the purchase of four new vending machines which will cost £36,000 to buy outright. It is estimated that they will have lives of seven years at the end of which their scrap value will be £1,000. To operate them an average investment in working capital of £3,000 will be required.

After depreciation of £5,000 per annum, the forecast operating profits are:

	£			£
Year 1	3,000	Year 2		3,000
2	4,000		6	2,000
3	5,000		7	1,000
4	5,000			

The company target rate of return on this activity is 10% after tax and discounting. The machines will qualify for 100% first year allowance in respect of tax and the company pays Corporation tax at the rate of 52%.

One manager supports the purchase because he has worked out the rate of return to be $18\frac{3}{4}\%$ as follows:

$$\frac{\text{Average annual profit}}{\text{Average investment}} \quad \frac{£3,286}{£17,500} \times 100$$

However, the after tax discounted rate is barely 10% worked out as follows:

Tax Calculations

Year	Operating profit £	Depreciation £	Pre-tax cash flows £	Capital allowance and charge £	Taxable profit £	Corporation Tax @ 52% £
1	3,000	5,000	8,000	36,000	(28,000)	—
2	4,000	5,000	9,000		9,000	(14,560)
3	5,000	5,000	10,000		10,000	4,680
4	5,000	5,000	10,000		10,000	5,200
5	3,000	5,000	8,000		8,000	5,200
6	2,000	5,000	7,000		7,000	4,160
7	1,000	5,000	6,000	(1,000)	7,000	3,640
8	—					3,640
	23,000	35,000	58,000	35,000	23,000	11,960

D.C.F. Calculations ( ) = cash outflows

(a) Operating cash flows

Year	Pre-tax cash flows £	Tax payable £	Post-tax cash flows £	10% P.V. factors £	Discounted cash flows £
1	8,000	—	8,000	0·91	7,280
2	9,000	14,560	23,560	0·83	19,555
3	10,000	(4,680)	5,320	0·75	3,990
4	10,000	(5,200)	4,800	0·68	3,264
5	8,000	(5,200)	2,800	0·62	1,736
6	7,000	(4,160)	2,840	0·56	1,590
7	6,000	(3,640)	2,360	0·51	1,204
8	—	(3,640)	(3,640)	0·47	(1,711)
	58,000	(11,960)	46,040		36,908

(b) *Investments Cash Flows*   10% P.V. factors

0	Machines	(36,000)	1·00	(36,000)	
	Working capital	(3,000)	1·00	(3,000)	
7	Machines – scrap	1,000	0·51	510	
	Working capital recouped	3,000	0·51	1,530	(36,960)
	Net present value @ 10%				– £52

Cost of Capital

One criticism of D.C.F. is that although a percentage rate of return is at the heart of the technique, there is no universal method of calculating a minimum or a target rate for projects in different organizations. D.C.F. tends to get singled out for this criticism but it applies to all percentage appraisal methods. Golden Hotels Project X50 (Exhibit 15–2) mentions a 6% cost of capital and 10% being a minimum planned rate. This second rate is subjective in that the company may set a different rate target for different investments based on various factors, for example risk involved, whether a replacement or an expansion project, and how desirable is the project. The first rate, the cost of capital, can be calculated in different ways giving broadly similar results. One way is to determine the cost of each course of capital and weighting each according to its proportion to total capital. For example 9% cost of capital would result from:

	Amount	Proportion	Source Cost	Weighted Cost
	(1)	(2)	(3)	(4)=(2×3)
	£	%	%	%
Ordinary shares – market value	100,000	66·67	11·0	7·33
10% Debentures (52% Tax)	50,000	33·33	4·8	1·60
	150,000	100·00		8·93
				9%

The cost of debentures is straightforward, being the gross amount less the current corporation tax percentage because the interest is allowable for tax purposes.

The cost of capital derived from the issue of ordinary shares and likewise of equity is a difficult concept and one about which little agreement exists in practice. One method which appears to be useful is a variation of the price earnings ratio namely, the best estimate of what average future earnings per share would be if the proposed capital expenditure were not made, relative to the current market price of the shares.

The marginal cost of capital is another concept, but this is not generally recommended. If a debenture issue were made to fund a particular capital project, the cost of the issue and interest payable less tax could be regarded as the marginal cost. The danger is that a project returning only the marginal cost might lower overall company profitability.

It should be borne in mind that as some projects may be for non profit making purposes, the minimum rate for profitable new work must well exceed the average return from all investments.

Uncertainty in investment projects

Because there can be no certainty that forecasts will be achieved, attempts are sometimes made to take uncertainty into account to help the decision maker. Some methods employed are:

1. Adjusting the basic cash flows.
2. Adjusting the rate required. A higher rate of return may be required from projects of higher than average risk.
3. Three level estimates. High, medium and low values of the estimated factors making up the cash flows are taken and rates of return are calculated based on the various combinations, giving optimistic, average and pessimistic estimates. These help the decision maker by showing up the possible extreme results.
4. Applying probabilities to factors. If probabilities are applied to factors such as sales, costs, etc., then the probability of various returns being achieved may be calculated. This is a sophisticated method used mainly in conjunction with a computer.
5. Sensitivity analysis. This term refers to a statement of the likely effects on the return of changes in the factors such as a 10% drop in sales, compared with the average forecast.

Yield or Net Present Value method?

Generally both methods lead one to reach the same accept or reject decision for they are variations of the D.C.F. technique. An advantage of the Yield method is that it is more easy to understand. The assessment of project X47 sounds better

        as (a) 12% rate of return
      than (b) N.P.V. of −£124 at 16%

Some companies use both methods although N.P.V. would seem to have the overall advantage if only one method is used.

A project such as Golden Hotels' project X50 which is assumed to be the sole capital project planned, needs to meet certain criteria laid down by the company in the form of cost capital and/or a target rate of return. Either Yield or N.P.V. will achieve this end.

Moving on to other common situations, there are two to consider:

(a) capital rationing
(b) mutually exclusive projects

Capital rationing is the term used in capital budgeting to indicate that an overall maximum is being included in a period's budget for capital expenditure and the company selects that combination of a number of investments which will maximize profit. The procedure for selection is to list projects in order of profitability and to accept the first say five projects which will use up the capital budgeted. One way to list them in order is by D.C.F. yield. However, there is a way without requiring the yield by a further simple calculation to the N.P.V. for each project, called the 'Profitability Index'. In respect of each project, this is the present value of future net cash flows divided by the initial cash outlay.

Projects A and B in Exhibit 15–4 (a) are for this purpose assumed to be two of say ten projects to be placed in order of profitability and it can be seen that B would be placed higher than A on the list. If the £15,000 outflow on B happened to use up the last sum in the budget then A would be rejected.

Exhibit 15–4 (a)

Project		Basic cash flows £	N.P.V. @ 25% £			Profitability Index	Yield
A	year 0	(35,000)	(35,000)	$\dfrac{40,727}{35,000}$	=	1·16	35%
	2	63,636	40,727				
			+5,727				
B	year 0	(15,000)	(15,000)	$\dfrac{18,824}{15,000}$	=	1·25	40%
	2	29,412	18,824				
			+3,824				

Exhibit 15–4 (b)

A–B	year 0	(20,000)	(20,000)	$\dfrac{21,903}{20,000}$	=	1·09	31%
	2	34,224	21,903				
			+1,903				

Two mutually exclusive projects are so called if the acceptance of one means the automatic rejection of the other. They may have similar or different outlays.

The choice between mutually exclusive projects is generally based on net present values and of A and B in Exhibit 15–4(a) A would be chosen as it produces the higher N.P.V. If 25% used for discounting is the cost of capital (albeit rather high), then A gives the higher absolute return over the cost of capital. As a further check that A is the better project, the incremental cash flows (Exhibit 15–4(b)) show that 31% will be gained on the extra £20,000, still above the 25% cost of capital.

The Yield may be compared with the N.P.V. method visually to show that at one point two projects will have the same N.P.V. – about 30·5% in the case of A and B. Exhibit 15–5 illustrates the result of sample N.P.V. calculations.

For the Yield and N.P.V. methods to hold good it is assumed that there is the opportunity for cash inflows to be reinvested at the Yield rate and the N.P.V. rate respectively. From the graph it is evident that for rates up to about 31%, project A ranks higher than B. At about 31% the projects have equal ranking, but above 31% B ranks higher than A.

Exhibit 15-5

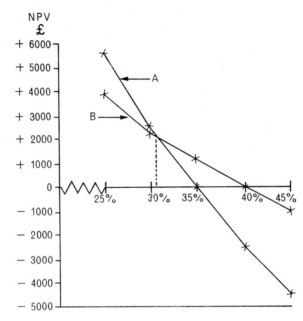

Table of Sample N.P.V. (£)

Project	Basic cash flows (0%)	25%	30%	35%	40%	45%
A year 0	(35,000)	(35,000)	(35,000)	(35,000)	(35,000)	(35,000)
2	63,636	40,727	37,545	35,000	32,454	30,545
N.P.V.s	28,636	5,727	2,545	Nil	(2,546)	(4,455)
B year 0	(15,000)	(15,000)	(15,000)	(15,000)	(15,000)	(15,000)
2	29,412	18,824	17,353	16,177	15,000	14,117
N.P.V.s	14,412	3,824	2,353	1,117	Nil	(883)

The graph also illustrates a method of determining the approximate Yield, for example A's Yield of 35% is where the N.P.V. curve cuts the horizontal axis after inserting points for 30% and 40%. It should be noted that curves rather than straight lines represent the changing N.P.V.s although with a narrow range of points about the Yield, 30% and 40% in this case a straight line would be sufficiently accurate.

Goodwill
Finding a value for goodwill by discounting future estimated profits was discussed in Chapter 13, and the method of calculating the discounted cash

flows should now be clear. Exhibit 13–3 showed proof that £5,130 was the calculated goodwill figure. The method of arriving at £5,130 by discounting is shown in Exhibit 15–6. This illustrates the point that if a choice exists between alternatives which cover a period of more than say two years, then D.C.F. can provide a more useful basis for decision making.

Exhibit 15–6

STATEMENT SHOWING DISCOUNTED PROFITS FROM
(a) PROPOSED PURCHASE OF RESTAURANT
(b) PROPOSED NEW RESTAURANT
DIFFERENCE REPRESENTING GOODWILL ON
PURCHASE OF RESTAURANT

End of year	Estimated profits from restaurant for sale	Present value factor @ 10%	Discounted Cash flow	Estimated profits from new restaurant	Present value factor @ 10%	Discounted Cash flow
	£		£	£		£
1	5,000	0·909	4,545	2,000	0·909	1,818
2	5,000	0·826	4,130	3,000	0·826	2,478
3	5,000	0·751	3,755	4,000	0·751	3,004
4	5,000	0·683	3,415	5,000	0·683	3,415
5	5,000	0·621	3,105	5,000	0·621	3,105
			18,950			13,820
			13,820			
Present value of increased profits from restaurant for sale at 10%			5,130			

D.C.F. Conclusion

The main work in any investment decision is forecasting the profit and cash flows expected to result from the project. D.C.F. is only a calculation applied to figures which should be in the hands of management anyway. With tables available the time taken to discount cash flows is short.

However, the problem does exist of management gaining sufficient understanding of the technique to have confidence in using it, which is basically a problem of education.

Questions and Problems

15–1 Why are capital investment decisions so important?

15–2 What do you understand by the term 'Net Present Value'?

15–3 Explain the following methods of capital investment appraisal:
(a) profit return on investment
(b) payback period
(c) discounted cash flow.

15-4   A company with £10,000 to invest internally has produced economic feasibility studies in respect of four projects whose life would in each instance be four years. The net annual cash flows are estimated as follows:

Projects

Years	A £	B £	C £	D £
1	Nil	Nil	5,000	20,000
2	Nil	5,000	5,000	3,000
3	15,000	5,000	5,000	1,000
4	15,000	10,000	5,000	1,000

The company borrows capital at 10% and expects a project to return 20%.

You are required to rank the projects in order of merit under the following methods of appraisal:

(a) payback

(b) average annual profit on investment

(c) average annual profit on average investment

(d) net present value at 10%

(e) net present value at 20%.

15-5   A catering organization is considering the purchase of a new washing-up machine at a cost of £80,000. It should save £16,000 in cash operating costs per year and has an estimated useful life of 8 years, with a zero disposal value.

You are required to calculate:

(a) the payback period;

(b) the net present value if the minimum rate of return desired is 10% and state with reasons whether or not the company should buy; and

(c) the D.C.F. yield.

15-6   The Brighton Horizon Co. Ltd., has £40,000 to invest. Out of the investment opportunities available, two have been selected for special attention. The immediate initial cash outlay for both is £40,000. It is forecast that for project A the net cash inflows arising from this investment will be:

Year	net cash inflows £
1	10,000
2	20,000
3	20,000
4	25,000

At the end of the 4th year the investment will be sold for £5,000.

For project B; net cost savings of £18,000 for each of the four years will be achieved.

You are required to:
(i) determine which project to recommend according to the
(a) pay back period method; and
(b) net present value method, assuming a discount factor of 20%
(ii) compare the payback period and net present value methods of investment appraisal.   (H.C.I.M.A.)

15–7 AM Co. Ltd. require a D.C.F. return of 15% or more on any capital project it undertakes. Three projects have been presented to the Capital Projects Committee for consideration, supported by the following projections:

			Projects X	Y	Z
			£	£	£
Expenditure	Year	0	10,000	15,000	20,000
Cash inflow	Year	1	3,000	11,000	10,000
		2	3,000	11,000	10,000
		3	3,000		10,000
		4	3,000		
		5	3,000		
		6	3,000		

Assuming only one project can be chosen, state which project you would choose and give your reasons.

15-8 The Golden Chain Restaurants have been buying Danish pastries from a baker at £0·04 each, but are now considering producing them themselves if this is likely to prove profitable.
    Two possible machines are available, A and B, and the costs in respect of each have been forecast as follows:

	Machines A	B
	£	£
Variable costs per pastry	·02	·0125
Fixed costs:		
Annual cash costs	2,500	3,500
Initial machine costs	6,000	15,000
Residual value at end of life	Nil	3,000
Estimated life of machine	4 years	4 years

You are required to:
1. Calculate how many pastries must be sold in order that total average annual costs equal the outside purchase costs in respect of each machine.
2. Calculate the annual number of pastries at which the cost would be the same whether produced on A or B machine.

3. Show which machine should be purchased on financial grounds if the annual sales forecast is 400,000 pastries, and the minimum desired rate of return is 10%.

15–9   The following information is given relating to a proposed capital expenditure project:

	£
Cost of project	350,000
Cash inflow per annum, prior to tax	80,000
Scrap/residual value	Nil
Working capital requirements:	
At commencement of project	10,000
After one year, a further	10,000
All released at end of the seventh year	20,000

Taxation assumptions:
   (*i*) corporation tax is at the rate of 50%;
   (*ii*) the first year allowance is at the rate of 100% and there are sufficient corporate profits available from other activities to absorb the whole amount of this allowance in the first year;
   (*iii*) tax payments are made and allowances are received in the year following that to which they relate.

Grant:
   A 20% tax free regional development grant is available and it is expected that this will be received one year after the purchase and installation of capital equipment.

Expected life of equipment	6 years
Company cut-off rate	18% after tax

You are required to:
   (*a*) compile a discounted cash flow (D.C.F.) statement to ascertain whether or not the project is acceptable;
   (*b*) calculate the approximate D.C.F. rate of return (internal rate of return) for the project.   (I.C.M.A.)

Further Reading

1. *Profitable Use of Capital in Industry,* I.C.M.A.
2. Lucey, T., *Investment Appraisal: Evaluating Risk and Uncertainty,* I.C.M.A.
3. Merrett, A. J. and Sykes, A., *Capital Budgeting and Company Finance,* Longmans Green & Co.
4. Wright, M. G., *Discounted Cash Flow,* McGraw-Hill.
5. Cox, B. and Hewgill, J. C. R., *Management Accounting in Inflationary Conditions,* I.C.M.A.

PRESENT VALUE TABLE

PRESENT VALUE OF £1 RECEIVED AT THE END OF n YEARS $\left(P = \dfrac{S}{(1+r)^n} \right)$

n	1%	2%	3%	4%	5%	6%	7%	8%	9%	10%	11%	12%	13%	14%	15%	16%
1	·99	·98	·97	·96	·95	·94	·93	·93	·92	·91	·90	·89	·89	·88	·87	·86
2	·98	·96	·94	·92	·91	·89	·87	·86	·84	·83	·81	·80	·78	·77	·76	·74
3	·97	·94	·92	·89	·86	·84	·82	·79	·77	·75	·73	·71	·69	·68	·66	·64
4	·96	·92	·89	·85	·82	·79	·76	·74	·71	·68	·66	·64	·61	·59	·57	·55
5	·95	·91	·86	·82	·78	·75	·71	·68	·65	·62	·59	·57	·54	·52	·50	·48
6	·94	·89	·84	·79	·75	·71	·67	·63	·60	·56	·53	·51	·48	·46	·43	·41
7	·93	·87	·81	·76	·71	·67	·62	·58	·55	·51	·48	·45	·43	·40	·38	·35
8	·92	·85	·79	·73	·68	·63	·58	·54	·50	·47	·43	·40	·38	·35	·33	·31
9	·91	·84	·77	·70	·64	·59	·54	·50	·46	·42	·39	·36	·33	·31	·28	·26
10	·91	·82	·74	·68	·61	·56	·51	·46	·42	·39	·35	·32	·29	·27	·25	·23
11	·90	·80	·72	·65	·58	·53	·48	·43	·39	·35	·32	·29	·26	·24	·21	·20
12	·89	·79	·70	·62	·56	·50	·44	·40	·36	·32	·29	·26	·23	·21	·19	·17
13	·88	·77	·68	·60	·53	·49	·42	·37	·33	·29	·26	·23	·20	·18	·16	·15
14	·87	·76	·66	·58	·51	·44	·39	·34	·30	·26	·23	·20	·18	·16	·14	·13
15	·86	·74	·64	·56	·48	·42	·36	·32	·27	·24	·21	·18	·16	·14	·12	·11

n	17%	18%	19%	20%	21%	22%	23%	24%	25%	26%	27%	28%	29%	30%	31%	32%
1	·85	·85	·84	·83	·83	·82	·81	·81	·80	·79	·79	·78	·78	·77	·76	·76
2	·73	·72	·71	·69	·68	·67	·66	·65	·64	·63	·62	·61	·60	·59	·58	·57
3	·62	·61	·59	·58	·56	·55	·54	·52	·51	·50	·49	·48	·47	·46	·44	·43
4	·53	·52	·50	·48	·47	·45	·44	·42	·41	·40	·38	·37	·36	·35	·34	·33
5	·46	·44	·42	·40	·39	·37	·36	·34	·33	·31	·30	·29	·28	·27	·26	·25
6	·39	·37	·35	·33	·32	·30	·29	·28	·26	·25	·24	·23	·22	·21	·20	·19
7	·33	·31	·30	·28	·26	·25	·23	·22	·21	·20	·19	·18	·17	·16	·15	·14
8	·28	·27	·25	·23	·22	·20	·19	·18	·17	·16	·15	·14	·13	·12	·12	·11
9	·24	·23	·21	·19	·18	·17	·16	·14	·13	·12	·12	·11	·10	·09	·09	·08
10	·21	·19	·18	·16	·15	·14	·13	·12	·11	·10	·09	·08	·08	·07	·07	·06
11	·18	·16	·15	·13	·12	·11	·10	·09	·09	·08	·07	·07	·06	·06	·05	·05
12	·15	·14	·12	·11	·10	·09	·08	·08	·07	·06	·06	·05	·05	·04	·04	·04
13	·13	·12	·10	·09	·08	·08	·07	·06	·06	·05	·04	·04	·04	·03	·03	·03
14	·11	·10	·09	·08	·07	·06	·06	·05	·04	·04	·04	·03	·03	·03	·02	·02
15	·09	·08	·07	·06	·06	·05	·04	·04	·04	·03	·03	·02	·02	·02	·02	·02

INDEX

ACCOUNTING AND FINANCIAL
MANAGEMENT IN THE HOTEL AND
CATERING INDUSTRY

Volume 1

Contents

Recording of Cash
Recording of Expenditure
Recording of Salaries and Wages
Recording of Income
Trial Balance
Preparation of Final Accounts
Accounting Adjustments – Routine and Year End
Depreciation, Replacement and Disposal of Fixed Assets
Incomplete Records
Accounts of Non-Profit Making Organizations
Accounts of Partnerships
Departmental Accounting
Mechanized Processing of Accounting Data

PRICE: £3·95